Embodying Lilith

-A Gnostic Kabbalah of Lilith-

Mark H. Williams

Circulos Tenebris Matrem Arcanas

www.Circulos-Matrem.com

Editing

Elizabeth Thomas and Adam Schlaegel

Art Credits

Cover - "The Tree of Lilith" by Tino Manning

Intro to Gnostic Kabbalah of Lilith – "Lilith with Fire Snake" by Misty Wood

Spheres – "Tree of Sorrows" By James McGee

Paths – by Lars Poyansky (Shutterstock)

For Brin – the most human being I ever met

FOREWARD

Lilith has had a splashy and colorful legacy—one in which she has worn many hats. After centuries of being inadvertently worshipped through fear and hatred, our current generation has begun reclaiming her with reverence and power. As devotees, it is our responsibility to use our voices to teach her ways of esoteric wisdom. Mark Williams has done just that with this book.

In 2019, I had the honor of meeting Mark and was invited into his home while on my own book tour in Columbus, Ohio. Walking into his home it was evident just how much it was more than a home, but also a Lilithian temple it is. The level of dedication he has towards Lilith vibrates throughout the space.

While Mark's work with Lilith is anchored in a different style than my own, it is abundantly evident that we not only work with but celebrate Lilith in all of her delicious delights. One of these main differences is the extensive Kabbalistic work Mark does with her, which is explored further in the pages ahead. In the 20 years that Lilith has been in my life, I have never been able to truly comprehend this aspect of her. I am thankful for our many chats in the past which have helped me to better understand what I could not before—and now have the documentation of it with this book. Mark's insight is presented in such a digestible manner that any seeker on Lilith's path, be they novice or advanced, will be able to take away valuable information for bonding, understanding, and honoring Lilith.

Becoming Lilith is an immaculate collection of passion, dedication, and creativity inspired by the legend that is Lilith. I am proud to be in an era where both Mark and I have been able to contribute to the demystification of Lilith's mysteries so that other seekers can find the solace of her dark light. This book is a mirror. May you see Lilith in yourself and amplify that energy to reflect in the world.

—Michael Herkes, author of The GLAM Witch: A Magical Manifesto of Empowerment with the Great Lilithian Arcane Mysteries

INTRODUCTION

When I wrote *Embracing Lilith,* I had no idea I would write anything more on the subject. However, as with everything, Lilith decides what she wants, and her followers usually learn to just go with it. Once the first book was published and the newness of having it finished was over, I started getting the inkling there might be another book in my future. My first attempt at laying out new topics looked far different from what this book has become. Initially I was somewhat set on continuing the same paradigm I had for the first book, with a section on history, a continuation of the myth, and then experiential topics. The big change from what I planned to what transpired came when Lilith told me "no myth." I feel like the myth in *Embracing Lilith* serves the purpose of helping readers get to know her. As they follow her journey, they hopefully begin to see that they themselves are not who they thought they were. Just as Lilith thought she had no purpose and had made all the wrong choices; she finds she has fulfilled her purpose all along. The same is true for all of us.

Embodying Lilith is much more about consciousness. It is about understanding we are on a journey to fulfill our spiritual evolution. Evolution is the core of who Lilith is – the conscious energy of change and transformation. So, in this book, instead of a myth, the focus is understanding Lilith's consciousness and in so doing, learning about our own. Through writing this book, I have come to know that the best way to change the world is to change ourselves. If we take up our true nature, our true purpose, and our true self, we can do anything. In this, we become Lilith.

I want to take this time to thank several people who have helped me on this journey. If not for Brandon, James, Tiffany, Elizabeth, Tino, Mike, the admins at Temple of Lilith, and, of course, my husband, Adam, I would not have had the vision or the energy to complete this. I also want to give a big thank you to Michael Herkes (author of Glam Witch) for such an amazing Forward for this book. My spiritual family is my muse, who energetically gives me the power and passion to create. I cannot thank you all enough for believing in me and listening as my rantings eventually turned into something somewhat coherent which could be put down on the page. Thank you all for being my sisters and brothers – we are truly Lilin and Lilu. Lots of love to you all.

PART 1

INTRODUCTION TO GNOSTIC KABBALAH OF LILITH

Introduction to Lilith

For those of you unfamiliar with Lilith, I will give a brief introduction. However, in my previous book, *Embracing Lilith,* I have a detailed section on Lilith's history, metaphysical connections, and even artistic representations of her through the ages. I will not be repeating all the details from *Embracing Lilith* but will include what I think is necessary to understand the new material we will cover in this book.

Lilith first appears in Sumerian literature as a semi-demonic goddess. Her name in the various Mesopotamian cultures are derivatives of Lili and Lilitu, meaning "of the air." She later appears in Judaic literature having several origins and descriptions. In addition to being considered demonic, she is also called the first wife of Adam. This comes from the fact Genesis 1 and 2 seem to provide two different accounts of creation. One features a woman created at the same time as Adam, and in the other the woman is created later from Adam's rib (or in a more accurate Hebrew translation, Adam's side). In Jewish *Midrash* (extra-biblical works), Lilith is the woman created at the same time as Adam and, of course, Eve is the one created from his "rib".

The mythos of Lilith has continued to this day and is now showing up in several different forms throughout popular culture. She appears as a symbol for women's liberation, a demoness, a goddess, and even a vampire in various fictional sources. In a lot of ways, it seems Lilith's day has come. She is more widely known and referenced now than at any previous time in history.

Kabbalah

The word Kabbalah means "to give," and has also been translated as "Tradition." The Kabbalistic tradition is an ancient form of Hebrew mysticism based on the *Torah* (the first five books of Hebrew Scripture which are part of the Christian "Old Testament"). Many people think Kabbalah was created in the 14th century, but this is not correct. Kabbalistic teachings go back into antiquity and are found in many different source works, probably starting as an oral tradition. The *Sefer Yetzirah (The Book of Formation)* was written around the 1st century CE but includes concepts that are much older. The *Sefer Zohar (The Book of Splendor)* first became known in 14th century Spain. This work is the progenitor of modern Kabbalah, but the tradition itself dates back far earlier.

The *Zohar* is a collection of 22 books comprised of discussions by rabbis on the nature of God, the Universe, and Humanity. The original text of the *Zohar* is mostly written in an obscure form of Aramaic. The writer was obviously not a native Aramaic speaker and vocabulary from medieval Spanish and Portuguese supplement the ancient language.

The author, Moses de Leon, claimed he found the texts and put them together into one integrated set; however, based on the text itself and comments from his widow, it is assumed by most scholars he wrote the whole series himself. In either case, the *Zohar* is a brilliant set of interwoven teachings incorporating common symbolism and theme throughout.

Kabbalah does not spring from thin air. The contents of Kabbalah, including the source works such as *Zohar*, are an expansion of Hebrew Scripture into its fullest meanings. Each letter in Hebrew does not just represent a sound, but a word and a number. This means when reading Hebrew texts, the inner, mystical meaning can be drawn out through considering the original text, the string of words from each letter, and the gematria (numerical values of words). Hebrew is a three-dimensional language, unlike English which is composed of letters which are merely sounds.

There have been several different glyphs used to help explain Kabbalistic ideas. In early Kabbalah, the system was depicted as spheres within spheres. This is a difficult way to look at the interactions of the energies, although probably a more accurate picture. The glyph used today was created in the 14th century and is commonly known as the Tree of Life. The glyph shows "God's energy" as it flows down from absolute indivisible divinity into tangible physical creation. We will discuss the Tree of Life later in this book.

Kabbalah, at its heart, is a complex set of ideas which are to be studied with a great deal of reflection and meditation. The teachings can be expanded into a magickal system for personal practice and group ritual. Kabbalah has been embraced and adapted by many other traditions including Hermeticism, Thelema, Golden Dawn, and other occult groups, and is used frequently within esoteric circles today.

Gnosis

The term *gnosis* is a Greek word meaning "knowledge." Since it is associated with spirituality, some have claimed the term means "hidden knowledge," but it is more accurate to define it as "experiential knowledge." Therefore, a true Gnostic is someone who seeks experiential understanding of their spirituality instead of relying upon blind faith. Faith is a good starting point for the journey, but it is never the Gnostic's end goal. Faith can be considered the "belief in experience yet to be had," and our journey is always faith which experience will transform into *gnosis*.

Gnosticism was first used to describe a group of mystical Christian traditions that existed around the second century CE. Some scholars have limited their definition to only these groups and have not considered the broader picture of what Gnosticism encompasses. Since a Gnostic seeks experiential knowledge of their spirituality, the term can be used in conjunction with other varied traditions around the world. There is no need to limit Gnosticism to the Christian stream. One could also consider Hinduism, Buddhism, Jewish Kabbalah, Taoism, Toltec tradition, ancient Druidism, Islamic Sufi tradition, some pagan traditions, and many other philosophies/religions to be of a Gnostic nature.

Because biased scholars consider the term Gnostic to only encompass Christian tradition which was considered heretical after the Council of Nicaea in the 4th Century CE, most of the world who know the term think all Gnostics hold the same beliefs. This is not the case. Just as there are many traditional Christian sects with a wide range of practices and beliefs, there is also a wide range of Gnostic traditions, including Pagan Gnostics.

Magick

The term magick may seem easy to define, but magick is really an extensive subject. The English word magic is derived from the ancient Persian word *magi.* It was later adopted into Greek and then Latin. The Latin use of the word was associated with demons and was deemed anti-Christian. Since the 19th century the term has taken on many meanings and been associated with any type of supernatural working and has lost some of its negative connotations because of the use of the term by stage magicians. For the purposes of this book, I will use the spelling magick to differentiate occult practice from stage magic. While some equate the 'k ending' with Alister Crowley, this information doesn't originate from his work.

I would define magick as a mystical or spiritual working focusing will and desire energy to make a change in reality. I know this is a broad definition, and it is meant to be. These changes can be physical or changes in consciousness; thus, they may or may not be visible manifestations. I apply the term magick to Kabbalah because any time you work within Kabbalah with intent, everything changes. Simply studying Kabbalah will change your consciousness and to a lesser extent, the consciousness of others around you. Once you take up Kabbalah as a practice, it will also allow you to alter other aspects of reality through your will and desire energy.

Magickal Kabbalah is an extremely powerful and transformative practice. What you do with this transformative power is vitally important. Most spiritual traditions include the concept of consequences for negative action. Because Kabbalah is based on our energy linking with that of other realms, taking negative action results in a backlash in both our consciousness and sometimes in our physical reality. It is never a good idea to invoke out of anger

or confused intention when working with Kabbalah. This is not to say protective magick, the binding of harmful energy, or even casting negative consequences on someone is never done, just be aware of how you are directing your intent.

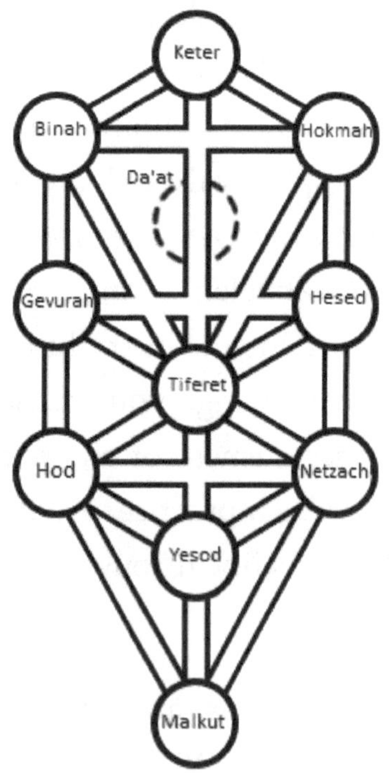

Tree of Life

The Tree of Life is first mentioned in Genesis 2:9 – "In the middle of the garden were the Tree of Life and the tree of the knowledge of good and evil." Adam and Eve are told not to eat of the fruit of the Tree of Knowledge of Good and Evil, but they are not told anything about the Tree of Life. It is not until after the fall that God states Adam and Eve must be barred from eating of the Tree of Life, so they do not have everlasting life. Some Kabbalists believe the Tree of Knowledge of Good and Evil and the Tree of Life are the same tree, and it is only after we partake of "individuality" from the forbidden tree that we can partake of eternal life.

In the 14th century, Kabbalists began using a glyph also called the Tree of Life. This glyph is a pictorial representation of how the divine light flows down from the sea of light where God Most High dwells (a place of total unity, no time, no space, and nothing we can understand while incarnate) down into creation. The Tree of Life glyph is made up of 10 spheres and 22 paths (and an 11th pseudo-sphere, which will be discussed later).

The Tree of Life can be divided into three pillars: Severity on the left, Mercy on the right, and Compassion in the middle. Each sphere, called *Sephirah* (plural *Sephirot*) in Hebrew, has several correspondences and represents the divine light as it manifests at different levels as it flows down into creation. The paths between the spheres are called *Netivah* (plural *Netivot*) in Hebrew and each corresponds with one of the 22 Hebrew letters, representing a level of consciousness connecting the spheres it spans. What needs to be noted is that the relationship between the spheres is extremely important. Legend says the original universe had no relationships, with spheres just lined up from top to bottom. The divine energy could not be contained, and the Tree shattered. It was only when relationships were created between the spheres balance could maintain the structure and form of the Tree.

Groupings of three spheres are called triads. The first, Supernal Triad, is made up of Spheres: *Keter, Hokmah, Binah.* The second, Moral Triad, includes Spheres: *Hesed, Gevurah,* and *Tiferet*. The third, Action Triad, contains Spheres: *Netzach, Hod,* and *Yesod. Malkut* is considered the fruit of the Tree and not part of any triad. As you can probably tell by the names of these groupings, the highest is the furthest from creation and the tenth sphere, the fruit, is actual creation and eventually physical reality. The 11th sphere is actually not a Sephirah, but instead a gateway between universes.

One thing that needs to be addressed is the different spellings of the Sephirot. You will see wildly different spellings of each sphere in different texts and on different images, this is because Hebrew has its own alphabet and when words are translated to English, they are transliterated to make the English letters produce the correct sounds. This means that the translation of letters is relative and can produce wildly different spellings. For instance, the Sphere Hesed may be spelled Chesed or other variations.

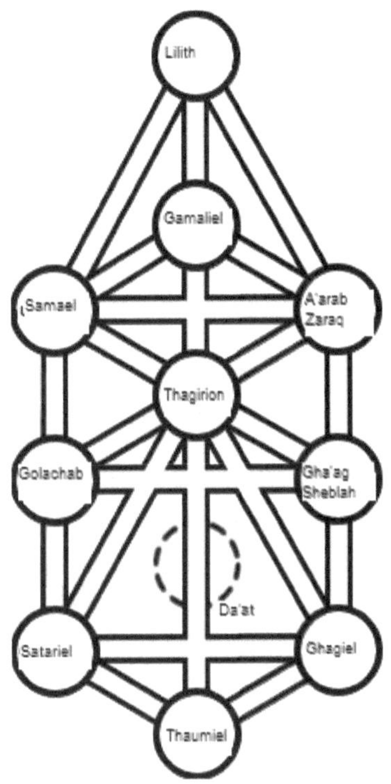

Tree of Shadows / Tree of Knowledge of Good and Evil

Each sphere also has a shadow side. This shadow is known as *Qlipah* (plural *Qlipoth*) in Hebrew. *Qlipoth's* literal meaning is "husks of darkness" referring to the aspect of each sphere having its energy masked and restricted through shadow. One of the goals of working with Kabbalah is for the magickal practitioner to heal and uplift their own shadow, as well as the shadow of other beings and that of the world.

The Tree of Shadows (also known as the Tree of Good and Evil or the Tree of *Qlipoth*) is sometimes considered the back side of the tree or the shadow of the Tree which lays below Kingdom (Malkut), the last Sephirah. In either case, the Tree of Shadows is very much a mirror of the Tree of Life. The Tree of Shadows is also called *Sitra Ahra,* The Other Side.

Some consider one Tree good and the other evil, but the differentiation is more about order and chaos. Reality is made of a combination of both conditions, and we need to integrate both opposing forces into ourselves. It is said the Tree of Shadows is the fast path to enlightenment because of its nature linking to our shadow selves. There are big rewards, but many obstacles to overcome on this "darker" path, because we can easily get trapped in our shadow. In my personal work, I use both Trees as a means to enlightenment.

Universes

The Tree of Life manifests in repeated linked succession through four different universes, or *Olamot* in Hebrew (singular is *Olam*). In other words, there are four "copies" of the Trees, each linked together with some overlap. The fifth universe is in a state of complete unification and thus no Tree of Life exists in this *Olam,* because there cannot be levels, pillars, or any other differentiation where everything is unified.

The Universes (*Olamot*) and their contents are as follows – from highest to lowest:

- *Adam Kadmon* (Complete Unification)
- *Atzilut* (Deity)
- *Beriyah* (Archangels, Archdemons, Archarchons)
- *Yetzirah* (Angels, Demons, Archons)
- *Assiyah* (Physical world)

Kabbalistic views on universes and dimensions are even more complicated because every sphere is said to have yet another Tree within it. This goes on for infinity, meaning there are universes within universes within universes.

Ain, Ain Sof, Ain Sof Or

Kabbalah teaches that creation emanates from a conscious force beyond time and space, where there is no duality, and everything is one. This non-place is called the following:

- *Ain* – No Thing
- *Ain Sof* – Eternity

- *Ain Sof Or* – Endless Light

The description of No Thing does not mean "nothing," but instead something which is no one thing and not like anything else because it is the primordial source. This is much like the Gnostic idea of *pleroma* (the All). This No Thing is called eternity because there is no beginning or end and described as endless light due to it being a unified conscious force which has no beginning or end.

The Zohar translates the first words of the *Torah,* "In the beginning, God created," as "With beginning created God." This sounds like a strange translation, but what it is saying is that with a beginning, a start of creation in time/space, this conscious force created "God" or deity. There was no God before this creation because all was unified, all was one, all was beyond. *Ain* generates personalities or gods and goddesses which form through the refraction of this energy as it passes into creation. The personalities of deity are called *Partzufim* (singular *Partzuf*).

Another interesting correlation is that the word *Ain* is spelled with the Hebrew letters *Ayin Yod Nun*. The word for "I" (first person singular) in Hebrew is *Ani – Ayin Nun Yod.* So, this No Thing of eternity becomes the individual who returns to the No Thing through the path of enlightenment.

The Soul

Just as there are five universes, there are also five levels of the soul in Kabbalah (similar to ideas of the soul in other cultures such as ancient Egyptian tradition). The soul is made up of the following manifestations:

Earthly Soul (*Nefesh*) – The *Nefesh* is the ego and personality. Often called "the flesh" in Christian scripture, this part of the soul burns off at death and usually disintegrates, although in some cases it becomes earthbound as a ghost. There are two forms of the Earthly Soul – The Bestial Soul (*Nefesh Behomet*) which is focused on ego, and The Enlightened Soul (*Nefesh Elokit*) which is focused on attaining the true or divine self.

Spirit (*Ruach*) – *Ruach,* meaning breath, is the human intelligence and the divine intelligence that are housed in a human body. The lower Spirit points toward the Earthly Soul and is our intelligence where the upper Spirit points toward the Eternal Soul and toward enlightenment.

Eternal Soul (*Neshamah*) –The *Neshamah* is the part of the soul that reincarnates from incarnation to incarnation. This is the true "us," which exists forever. What can be kept (from *Nefesh Elokit, Ruach,* and *Neshamah*) stays from one incarnation to the next. This aspect of the soul is asleep until we reach some level of spiritual realization, and then it awakens.

Life Force (*Hayyah*) –The *Hayyah* is the part of the soul which connects the aspects that dwell in the body (Earthly Soul, Spirit, and Eternal Soul) with the aspects which extend outside of creation (all the way into the universe of *Adam Kadmon*).

Divine Spark (*Yechidah*) – The *Yechidah* is the part of every being which exists beyond creation and is completely integrated into the divine realm. When this aspect of the soul is completely awake, a being reaches full enlightenment and liberation.

Creation

Kabbalistic creation myth speaks of the No Thing (*Ain*) desiring to create. In this primordial will for creation, the No Thing pulls back the Endless Light (*Ain Sof Or*) and creates a womb for creation to exist, separate from No Thing, Eternity, and Endless Light. This restriction of God-self is called the *Tzim-Tzum*. In this womb, light flows down and becomes the Spheres (*Sephirot*) and Paths (*Netivot*) of the four lower universes. With each universe the light becomes more restricted and more physical until it gets to our universe and the Earth. The Shadow or Husks for all these spheres of light is the *Qlipoth* of the Tree of Shadow.

Eventually, when all souls are brought back to the light – either in conscious or unconscious unity, the universes will roll back up and rejoin the Endless Light. The restriction (*Tzim-Tzum*) will collapse. Kabbalah teaches that as soon as this happens, another restriction will occur, and another set of universes and creation will be emanated; this will happen over and over for all Eternity.

Aspects of Deity

As the light flows down through the universes and becomes more and more restricted, the light takes on various aspects or restrictions of the No Thing. The No Thing is, as stated before, like nothing in creation, but somehow everything and more at the same time. So as this light flows into more restricted universes, it takes on different characteristics at each of the Spheres.

In the highest Universe, *Adam Kadman*, there is no differentiation, time, space, or anything separate from unified divinity. This is as close to the No Thing as it gets, so there is nothing to discuss regarding Spheres. However, as the light flows into the next four universes, the light takes on forms increasingly closer to those of our experience.

In the second universe, *Atzilut,* the light becomes different personalities of deity (*Parzufim*) and names of deity. In Jewish Kabbalah, this means specific personalities and names that are used in Hebrew Tradition. In our paradigm of magickal Kabbalah, the personalities and names are any deities and their roles within the Godhead. It must be noted these gods and goddesses in Kabbalah are emanations of the light restricted in the second universe, so they are part of the light, yet separate and distinct personalities. It is possible for humans to take any of these personalities and warp their messages and intent so what is portrayed and seen are no longer true aspects of the light, but instead entities created in our image. This is what Gnostics called *Demiurge* (false creator).

The third universe, *Beriyah,* is the universe of Archangels, Archdemons, and Archarchons. As the light restricts here, it becomes powerful beings of mercy (Archangels), beings of severity (Archdemons) and beings of admixture (Archarchons). These beings are all necessary for the evolution of souls, free will, and the balance of creation. Each one serves a purpose and given enough time and experience they will individuate and find enlightenment.

The fourth universe, *Yetzirah,* is the universe of Orders of Angels, Orders of Demons, and Orders of Archons. The restriction of the light breaks up the large Arch-beings into multitudes of their kind. These are again all necessary and part of the creation cycle.

The fifth universe, *Assiyah,* is the universe of physical creation. The light restricts to a point at which it makes planets, moons, stars, and cosmic cycles within creation. It must be mentioned that Kabbalah teaches these manifestations are different depending on where in the universe you are located and the Tree morphs depending on the planetary system. All of the possibilities inherent in this teaching form way too big a discussion for the scope of this book, but their existence points to the enormity of Kabbalah and the Universe.

Each Sphere of the Tree of Life represents "aspects of deity"--whether divine personalities, arch-beings, orders, or planetary bodies within each of the four lower universes. Kabbalah is a map of how these energies manifest, connect, and can be used to grow our consciousness and our magickal practice. Part 2 of this book will delve into the Spheres individually, and how to work with each of them.

In Kabbalah personalities of deity are call *Partzuf* (plural *Partzufim*). These personalities are aspects of the same energy at different spheres and levels of the Tree. Even though these personalities are from the same conscious energy doesn't mean that they can't or shouldn't be treated as separate identities with their own personalities and desires.

Paths

The twenty-two paths (Netivot) on the Tree, as stated previously, are represented by the twenty-two Hebrew letters and by the imagery of the Major Arcana of the Tarot. The paths are levels of consciousness which connect the Spheres, moving from one to the next and creating an energy intelligence through their flow. Again, Hebrew is considered a multi-dimensional language in which every letter has a meaning and a number associated with it. These letters represent a primordial energetic language; this language's energy and vibration composes everything in all universes, as the energy flows down from the universe of *Adam Kadmon*.

By studying the letters and the imagery of the Tarot, the practitioner can understand these energies and the relationships between the Spheres; the consciousness of God, the universe, and themselves; and give themselves a working guide for meditation and magick. Part 3 of this book will cover the Paths and give the reader ideas on how to work with them.

The Tarot

If you live in Western society, you probably have heard of Tarot cards. Most people, because of the media, associate them with card readings used to "tell the future." While the

Tarot can be used to do a reading that involves past, present, and future, the process is not one of simply pulling cards to give you this week's lottery numbers. And, in fact, the cards can be used for many different purposes beyond a reading, including meditation and as a guide to higher consciousness.

The Tarot deck was designed as a set of playing cards first used in mid-15th century Europe. Sources say they were not used for divination or any occult purpose until the 18th century. A deck consists of two different card types – the major and minor arcana. The minor arcana eventually evolved into the playing cards used today for poker, solitaire, and various other games. In the Tarot the minor arcana consists of cards 1(Ace)-10, Page, Knight, Queen, and King of four suits – pentacles, wands, cups, and swords. The major arcana consists of twenty-two picture cards, each of which has a distinctive image illustrating the card's title. These cards are not present in modern playing card decks.

Even though it is claimed the Tarot was not designed for anything but games, there is an uncanny correspondence between the Tarot and Kabbalah. The minor arcana reflects the ten *Sephirot* (*Keter* down to *Malkut*) and the four major *partzufim* or personalities of deity (daughter, son, mother, and father). The major arcana numbers twenty-two which matches both the number of letters in the Hebrew Alef-*Bet* and the number of paths in the Tree of Life. Modern

Kabbalists often use the major arcana to represent these paths as the levels of consciousness moving through the Tree.

Each card of the major arcana has a Hebrew letter associated with it, a key number (0 to 21), a numerical value based on Hebrew Gematria, and the imagery associated with the individual card. It is important to remember in Hebrew every letter has a meaning, unlike the Alphabet in English, and the Hebrew letters also serve as numerals. In English, the letters simply represent sounds, but in Hebrew the letter is a sound, a word in and of itself, and a number. This is not a numerological association in which letters are simply given a value, but a concrete identity correspondence in which the number is written using the ancient Hebrew letters. To understand the consciousness associated with the Tarot card, we must understand the letter's meaning, its gematria (numerical value), its association with other words, and the imagery the card displays. Some Hebrew letters have a different appearance and a different numerical value based on whether the letter is the final letter of a word or not. There are also three types of Hebrew letters – mother letters (representing primordial air, water, and fire), double letters (with dual sounds and meanings), and single letters.

The last section will discuss how to use the Hebrew letters and levels of consciousness represented by the Tarot's major arcana to align with our spiritual journey. Each entry will include practices and meditations to assist us, giving us the power to both embody Lilith and become our true selves. In the practices there will also be experiential tools to help understand how the energy of the card's imagery pertains to Lilith in each letter/card combination.

Evolution

Several months ago, I found myself researching the evolution of life on earth and then the evolution of hominids, culminating in the development of modern humans. I spent hours and hours reading and exploring evolutionary theory and the winding road leading to *Homo sapiens*. I kept asking myself, why am I looking into this so deeply? Sure, it was interesting, but outside my normal spiritual contemplations. But somehow, I could not stop myself, and I explored a wide range of ideas.

You may wonder what evolution has to do with a book on Lilith and be tempted to skip this part. Bear with me and keep reading, because this is integral to my view of Lilith and to what I believe she wants from us.

After a couple months of research, my exploration of evolution on Earth felt complete. Soon afterward, I had a dream in which Lilith came to me and said, "I Am Evolution!" When I awoke, I was a little confused by her statement, but after some contemplation and reviewing of my notes, it started to make sense. We must remember what Lilith's name means in Hebrew. As stated in *Embracing Lilith,* her name is composed of the letters *Lamed Yod Lamed Yod Tav. Lamed Yod* means "That which drives to the Spirit of God" and *Tav* means "unification," so she is the force which drives us to unification with who we truly are.

Currently scientists believe life started on earth about 3.77 billion years ago, in the primordial soup of the early planet. This life took on more and more complex forms until the seas were filled. The earth went through several cycles with amphibians, lizards, and then dinosaurs ruling over the land. Each of these "ages" occurred because of catastrophe such as giant volcanos, changes in climate, and eventually a giant comet.

Sixty-five million years ago a comet hit the earth causing a massive climate change and wiping out most of the world's terrestrial animal population. The large dinosaurs all perished, and it became the time of mammals and birds. Both were able to flourish and take over every corner of the earth.

Both mammals and birds were able to evolve larger brains that have given them an advantage to this day.

Primates eventually evolved, and about 4.4 million years ago our earliest human ancestors left their jungles and took to the grassy plains of Africa. These creatures were just over three feet-tall and were not extremely far removed from other apes; these human relatives only had a brain size of 350-515 cc, compared to a modern chimp (our closest living relative) with a brain size of 320-430 cc. However, they began to walk upright to see over the grasses and avoid predators.

Over time several prehuman species evolved. Some are direct ancestors of humans, some interbred with those that would evolve into the modern human population even though their surviving genetic contribution was not large enough for them to be considered our direct ancestors. Yet other species died out and left no contribution to modern human DNA. No one knows for sure why brain sizes increased, but brains got bigger and bigger and gained more complexity until anatomically modern humans appeared in Africa about 195,000 years ago. Since then, human evolution has continued in the face of challenges such as massive changes in climate, including an ice age. We have competed for food and shelter against various predators that could have easily wiped out our ancestors. However, with brain size increases that brought us to a present capacity of approximately 1260 ccs, humans as a species began to dream, imagine, create, and have self-awareness. Language, spirituality, and art all come from a bigger brain, one which gives us the ability to understand and transmit knowledge.

The point to the preceding paragraphs is that evolution does not just happen in a linear progression in perfect circumstances. In fact, it seems evolution takes place through fits and spurts, occurring with dramatic jumps in the middle of chaos. Whatever the details are surrounding the rise of humans to earth, one thing is for certain, it would not have happened without challenges and obstacles pushing us along our evolutionary progress. In no way am I proposing we are done with evolution, either. I believe our next step in evolution is spiritual; raising our consciousness to higher levels will eventually bring us to our true destiny.

When Lilith told me she is Evolution, I do not believe she was being vague or metaphorical. I think she is literally the embodiment of the circumstances in the world and the drive within us seeking to move forward to our destiny. Our survival as a species will be dependent on our next jump in consciousness. We must break free from the egoistic desires for power and control and be able to embody our true nature. Lilith's myth is all about taking control of one's darkness, integrating it into our whole, and using this force to evolve into a true spiritual being.

Shadow vs. Darkness

In Western culture we are frequently stuck in dualism. We tend to think of everything in terms of opposites, such as "good" and "bad." This comes out of the influence of Zoroastrianism on Christianity. When the Romans destroyed the second Temple in Jerusalem and dispersed the Jewish people (around 70 CE), early Christianity also spread into various areas of the Empire. One of the main religious movements influencing most of the Near East at that time was based on the teachings of the Prophet Zoroaster. These teachings focus on a God of Light and God of Darkness who are in eternal conflict. The formalized Christian New Testament did not yet exist – the canon was not locked down until the 4th Century CE – and many Christians synchrotized other religions into their faith. The Zoroastrian dualistic view began to take hold in Christianity, and doctrine began to focus on the God of the Bible and his son Jesus representing the God of Light in an eternal war with the "God" of Darkness, Satan. In Jewish Tradition, however, the Satan is an accuser. The book of Job shows Satan in the throne room of God, asking permission from *Yahweh* to tempt Job. There is no "war" or "struggle"; instead, *Yahweh* is all powerful and the Satan serves a purpose within creation. When Emperor Constantine converted to Christianity and made it the state religion of the Holy Roman Empire, this borrowed concept of light and darkness in total opposition came into Europe with it and eventually spread throughout the world. Modern day Western culture owes its dualistic view of reality to the Zoroastrian influence on early Christianity.

Non dualistic spiritual tradition does not think of Light and Dark as opposites, or as one being good and one being bad. They are instead both on the same continuum of experience, in balance and keeping the universe moving toward its ultimate purpose. In Kabbalah, light is associated with *Hesed*, "mercy," which is abundance. This light is "good," but without balance the light would consume creation and everything would roll back up to its source – the "No Thing). Darkness is associated with *Gevurah*, "severity," which is restriction. Without balance, darkness brings separation and entropy. However, when the light and dark are balanced, then creation has time to evolve and change. Kabbalah is all about balancing light and dark, mercy and severity, into what is called compassion, the compromise between the two.

What we confuse with darkness and consider evil is actually shadow. The shadow is a false reflection of something. If we look at the analogy of the sun shining down on an object and then a false image of the object cast against the ground or a wall, we see the shadow is not light, but it is not really darkness either. Instead, it is a distortion. Our shadow never looks exactly like us. Depending on the angle of the light shining on it, the shadow is elongated or shrunken. It is also two-dimensional instead of a fully formed likeness. I see this "shadow" as the egoistic state of beings when they are only seeing a partial truth. They believe or act in a two-dimensional false reflection of the truth they are seeing. This reflection is not Light or Dark. Our Spiritual evolution is to learn from the Light and Dark, casting aside the shadow self so we can be more fully who we really are.

Consciousness and Embodiment

The Kabbalistic myth cycle seen in Jewish and Christian scripture depicts humans in the form of Adam and Eve as starting out in unconscious unity with God. This means humanity (and all life) has always been emanations of the sea of consciousness manifesting as divinity within Creation. But this unity, because it is unconscious, allows for no true individuality in these human archetypes. The parable of them eating the fruit of the Tree of Knowledge of Good and Evil illustrates that humanity had to gain a sense of duality and separation from one another to become individuals. Without this awareness of duality, there is no true experience apart from the primordial Light. All animals, including humans, that have any self-awareness also have some degree of feeling separated, because the concepts of *I, them, us,* and *we* become part of our experience as we individuate. This is necessary, because without this seeming separation there is no drive for change or growth.

Kabbalah teaches that once a species reaches individuation, its members can each then choose to return to the Endless Light of Consciousness aware and whole. This is said to be the whole point of creation. Over the course of billions of years, all individuals reach their fulfillment via the enlightenment process and then return their experience to the collective consciousness, bringing all life in the Cosmic Cycle along with them.

In Kabbalistic teachings we have the concept of multiple levels of the soul. All beings have five levels of their soul: *Nefesh* (ego), *Ruach* (intelligence), *Neshamah* (eternal soul), *Hayyah* (connection back to the light realm), and *Yechidah* (the part of every being which remains outside of time and space, still in the sea of light). Human psychology recognizes this idea in the three levels of consciousness. The *Nefesh* and lower *Ruach* are associated with the conscious mind, the upper *Ruach* and *Neshamah* are associated with the subconscious mind, and the *Hayyah* and *Yechidah* are associated with the super consciousness shared by all. Enlightenment is the process of linking and unifying the conscious, unconscious, and super conscious mind. This is the product of human and non-human evolution.

Lilith, being the force and consciousness of evolution, desires to push us forward in any way necessary so that we embody our full potential. This means we must examine and integrate our dark side, learning to accept all aspects of ourselves as a cohesive whole. Lilith is seen as a Dark Mother and even sometimes as a demon because this process can be extremely painful and seem like destruction. Our ego is averse to the process until it realizes the exploration is in its best interest and will not bring about its demise. We need to finally embrace Lilith within us and become our own force of evolution.

Shadow Work

There is a term often used in mysticism called the Dark Night of the Soul. This is an event in which the seeker begins to find answers, but those answers upset everything in their life and contradict their beliefs. This often causes a crisis; the person feels emotionally broken, depressed, and unsure of where to go from there. From experience, I know the Dark Night of the Soul is agony. It feels awful and often makes us believe there is nothing left for us and no recourse but to give up. However, the Dark Night of the Soul is a positive movement in our spiritual evolution. It means that what we thought of the world and of ourselves has become outdated and we need to find a new worldview. This is not the end, but the beginning.

This event is the one telling us we are ready to transcend death. Our ego sees this lack of clarity and structure as a form of death and so it rebels, causing all the pain and doubt we feel. The path forward is in rebuilding our understanding from the ground up. We must push aside old ideas and societal norms to take up who we really are.

Shadow work is the process of looking at our beliefs, experiences, and even our personalities to find those things which are egoistic constructs rather than real pieces of who we are. Everything about ourselves must be on the table for examination, and everything must be open for change, or the shadow work will be incomplete, and we will fall back into a Dark Night. Lilith is the conscious force of shadow work. She is the embodiment of the roller coaster of change we really need to discover our true path. This is why she is so scary to many people, and why she is considered "evil" by those who don't understand her. She will turn everything in your life upside down to root out a misplaced belief or anything else that is not true to your real nature.

To find true and lasting change which puts us on a path of enlightenment, we must let Lilith in to do her work. We must give her free rein to change anything needing alteration. This process is not about being "good," but instead being who we really are with no "programming" from society and our past.

Aspects and Consorts

In the Jewish *Midrash,* Lilith is syncretized with a couple of other female "demons" said to be her sisters or daughters. These beings are Na'amah, whose name means "pleasant"; and the elusive Agrat bat Mahlat, meaning "daughter of Mahlat." Both Na'amah and Agrat are called demons but are also associated with human women. *Midrash* declares Na'amah to be the sister of Tubal-Cain and the wife of Noah, while Agrat is the daughter of Mahlat (who is the daughter of Ishmael).

The myths are filled with stories of Lilith, Na'amah, and Agrat all being consorts to archdemons such as Samael and Ashmedai (Asmodeus), as well as humans such as Adam and Solomon. All three female beings share several traits and behaviors. What is even more confusing are the references to an ongoing enmity between Lilith the Elder and Lilith the Younger. In *Embracing Lilith,* I explore these myths and provide information about all four of these entities. What I want to explore in this text is their relationship to each other.

In most world religions, moon goddesses are usually seen as having a triple aspect, reflecting the phases of the moon and the different stages of womanhood--Maiden, Mother, Crone. However, there is often an overarching archetype which is the complete form of the Goddess. This can be seen in the imagery and mythos surrounding the

Greco-Roman deity, Hecate. She is often depicted in three guises which come together into the supernal Hecate.

Lilith is also associated with the moon. Her name is, of course, based in the Sumerian word for wind, "Lil," but in Jewish *Midrash* Lilith is the dark aspect of *Shekinah* (God's Presence and Power) discussed in detail as the moon in metaphor. These points me toward viewing these aspects of the dark feminine as all parts of a whole, centered on mysteries of the moon. Lilith the Elder, Lilith the Younger, Na'amah, and Agrat are all considered night queens who rule over the dark, just as the moon rules the night sky.

I would liken Na'amah to maiden, Lilith the Younger to mother, and Agrat to crone. Lilith the Elder then represents the supernal, enlightened synthesis of the other three. My reasoning for this classification is that Na'amah is pictured as a beautiful seductress enticing men into sin, making her an archetype for the youthful aspect and the waxing moon. Lilith the Younger is the consort of Ashmedai, king of the Shedim––human souls who never received bodies because of the Sabbat-who prey on mortal weakness. She is also the aspect of Lilith who is considered Mother of Demons, and thus fits the mother aspect of the full moon. Agrat, even though said to be the youngest, is always described as a hag. She is said to disguise herself in a glamour of beauty and seduce men before eventually revealing her aged, hideous appearance.

She is also the most wrathful aspect from all accounts, so I associate her with the Crone and the waning moon.

Lilith the Elder would then correspond with the dark moon, the hidden aspect of the Mother who is the totality of the other three personas. At different times she is stated to be consort to Samael, the Poison of God and most infamous demon, and to *Yahweh,* God most High. This seeming duality of her being the wife of what was considered evil incarnate and paired with the God of all creation points to the truth that she transcends light and dark, being the mother of everything: light, dark, and in between.

This myth cycle and its correlations with moon cycles points to Lilith being the dark aspect of Mother God, inseparable from the light once she transcends creation and enters the supernal realm. From a Kabbalistic perspective, Na'amah would be the avatar of *Malkut,* Kingdom, and the dark Daughter or Bride. Lilith the Younger would be the avatar of *Yesod,* Foundation, as well as *Tifferet,* Beauty, with Lilith the Elder as the avatar of *Binah,* Understanding, and the Dark Mother. Agrat would be the avatar of *Gevurah,* Severity, and the dark Crone who rules over chaos and destruction. As the name Lilith in Hebrew (*Lamed Yod Lamed Yod Tav* – that which drives us to deity and ends in unification) indicates, in her aspects she is the force which pushes us to our highest potential by making us look at our own darkness and anger. She pushes us until we deal with everything within us and integrate it into wholeness. Once we have reached the point of integration, Lilith the Elder, mistress of *Da'at*, Experiential Knowledge and gateway to eternity, becomes our guide to enlightenment and unity. There are bright corollaries to these Dark aspects of the Mother, but they are outside the scope of this book.

What this means is that Lilith is the embodiment of the force of enlightenment. We can tap into this force and find transformation. We can approach her no matter what point we have reached in our journey, and gain insight and assistance. As I stated in *Embracing Lilith,* this is not an easy process and once you decide to go down this path, be ready for a wild ride. Lilith will force every hidden aspect of your life and personality to the surface and make you deal with each one. Her darkness is all knowing, and seeps into every crack in our armor. Life will be turned upside down, but you will eventually find peace and acceptance in her wings.

Wife of Adams

As I discussed in *Embracing Lilith,* one of the main Jewish concepts of Lilith is of her as Adam's first wife before Eve is separated from his side. This comes from the seemingly contradictory creation stories in Genesis 1 and Genesis 2.

Genesis 1 states that man and woman are created in God's image, but then Genesis 2 describes Adam alone with no mate. In this version, God pulls Eve from Adam (in English by removing his rib) so he will have a wife. In Jewish *Midrash* the question arises, if there was a woman in Genesis 1, what happened to her in Genesis 2? Rabbis explain this in *Midrash* by saying Adam's first wife was Lilith, but she resented his wanting to dominate her, so she called out the secret name of God and left Eden and went to the land of Nod.

The famous rabbi Isaac Luria, considered the father of modern Kabbalah, wrote: "it is said there are many Liliths, but the greatest of these is the wife of *Adam Kadmon*, a being who God used as an avatar to create the Universe in all its dimensions." This is quite a dramatic statement. *Adam Kadmon* is not the original human named Adam, but instead the *partzufim* (personality) of primordial perfect being who is the highest universe of total unity in Kabbalah. One may ask, how the greatest aspect of Lilith is the avatar of all the universes and consort of the primordial perfect being? She is the conscious force which propels mankind to this perfected state of unification. It is obvious from Luria's comments that he saw her as a multidimensional being with many facets. This view helps make sense of the many myths about Lilith and how they seem to contradict her nature.

Lilith in the Garden of Eden and the Land of Nod

In Kabbalah there is no heaven or hell as traditional Christians think of them. There are seven heavens and seven hells. None of these are permanent locations for the soul, but temporary afterlife states in which souls work through karma. The seven heavens correspond to the first seven Spheres of the Tree of Life (located one sphere up the Tree from each other) and the seven hells correspond to the first seven *Qlipoth* of the Tree of Shadows.

Lilith was created and placed in the Garden of Eden. Eden is located in the first Heaven, a virtual paradise, located in *Yesod*. Eden in Hebrew is spelled *Ayin Dalet Nun*. *Ayin* means foundation, *Dalet* door, and *Nun* human soul (ego and eternal soul). The Hebrew for Eden shows that its purpose is to take the foundation of a being and transform it into a human soul. This is the purpose of the Tree of Knowledge of Good and Evil. The "fruit" causes the transformation into an individual with an ego. Lilith arises in Eden, but she can transform, finding individuation without eating from the tree. Her anger at Adam helps her to see she is more than she thought, and she speaks the secret name of God, leaving Eden.

Midrash says she travels to the land of Nod. Nod is in the first Hell, located within the *Qlipoth* of *Gamaliel*. In Hebrew, Nod is spelled *Nun Yod Dalet*. *Nun* is again the human soul, *Yod* represents the spirit of divinity, and *Dalet* is door. The purpose of Nod is different than Eden. It takes a human soul, joins it with the spirit of divinity and gives it transformation. The question is, transformation into what? Since this transformation is not specified, the principle would be transformation into whatever the soul wants to be.

The journey from Eden to Nod and beyond is one which Lilith took. Adam never took this journey, so he stayed a human soul. Lilith on the other hand, chose to be more through sheer force of will. This is who she is, and how she begins in the myth cycle as a human woman and becomes a goddess.

Lilith and the Huluppu Tree

In the *Epic of Gilgamesh,* Lilith is said to have made her house in a huluppu tree which Inanna wants to make furniture from but cannot. Lilith is living in it, a snake has taken up residence at the root, and a Zu bird is in its branches. So, Inanna goes to her brother (another god), and he has Gilgamesh go fix the situation.

Inanna is called the joyful one, Goddess of Love and War. Lilith is called the Maiden of Desolation and we know at this time she is considered a storm goddess to the Sumerians. There is much rich imagery in this story. Though today's Kabbalah would not have been present at this time in Sumeria, one can still see its parallels to this story. I believe the huluppu tree can represent the Tree of Shadows consisting of Qlipoth.

The snake in the roots of the tree is reminiscent of the snake in the garden. In *Midrash,* Eden's snake is Lilith in a serpent form. The huluppu snake could reference Lilith in her more physical form as Na'amah at the base in the *Qlipoth* called Lilith. Lilith then resides in the rest of the tree, from *Gamaliel* through *Satariel.* At the top of the tree is a Zu bird. The Zu bird in Sumerian religion is associated with a god who stole the tablets of destiny to become all-knowing. The Zu bird and the god it represents could be equated with Lucifer. As an angel, Lucifer is winged. He is said to have rebelled against God but is also called Light Bearer. Zu stole the tablets from the other gods and is cast out, just like Lucifer.

When Gilgamesh comes and sends the snake, Lilith, and the Zu bird away, he is clearing the husks of the Qlipoth for Inanna to use, metaphorically the Tree of Shadows becomes the Tree of Life, making this a myth of enlightenment and transformation.

Gender and Sexuality

I feel that it is important to call out a note on gender and sexuality at this point. Kabbalah and the myths about Lilith all conform to a male/female gender identity and to hetero-normative sexuality. All the source texts emerge from times and cultures that did not focus on gender identity and LGBT+ community. In fact, some of them were downright hostile to such concepts. This does not mean that Lilith would ever have an issue with anyone's gender identity or sexual orientation. In fact, quite the opposite. Lilith wants everyone to be as authentically themselves as possible, and this means acknowledging and claiming your gender identity and your sexuality.

I have seen many posts online about how Lilith only accepts women as her devotees. I believe everyone has the right to their own spiritual beliefs, but my experience is that she accepts everyone as long as they are willing to do the work of transformation and not judge others for their personal identity. If you are called to her and you love her, do not let anyone tell you that anything is going to limit your relationship.

It is true women hold an important place in Lilith's heart, because they have been oppressed, demeaned, and vilified in society for thousands of years. It is no accident Lilith represents as a woman most in most cases. She is the goddess of the oppressed and marginalized, and so female form is a perfect manifestation for her to take. However, Lilith is a force of empowerment for all.

I also want to call out that Kabbalah uses the term male to mean active and giving, while female means passive and receiving. Whether this was meant as a comment on gender or not, it is not how I use the terms. When Kabbalah was brought forth as a tradition, the common people knew little science and certainly no particle physics. If they had, the terminology would probably have been different. The only thing they knew was male herd animal put tab A into female herd animal slot B, and baby animals were created. The Kabbalists were amazingly knowledgeable in metaphysics, but they used language based on what they had experienced. I do not in any way believe that male and female beings are divided into givers and receivers. I believe that humans are a wide variety of male and female characteristics, and in fact, this binary description of gender and sexuality is outdated. So, if I use the terms male and female in a Kabbalistic manner, they are about polarities and not about types of people. I use the old terminology because if you read any other book on Kabbalah, it will use this way of discussing the subject. It is important to have that understanding before trying to read any of those texts.

PART 2

SPHERES

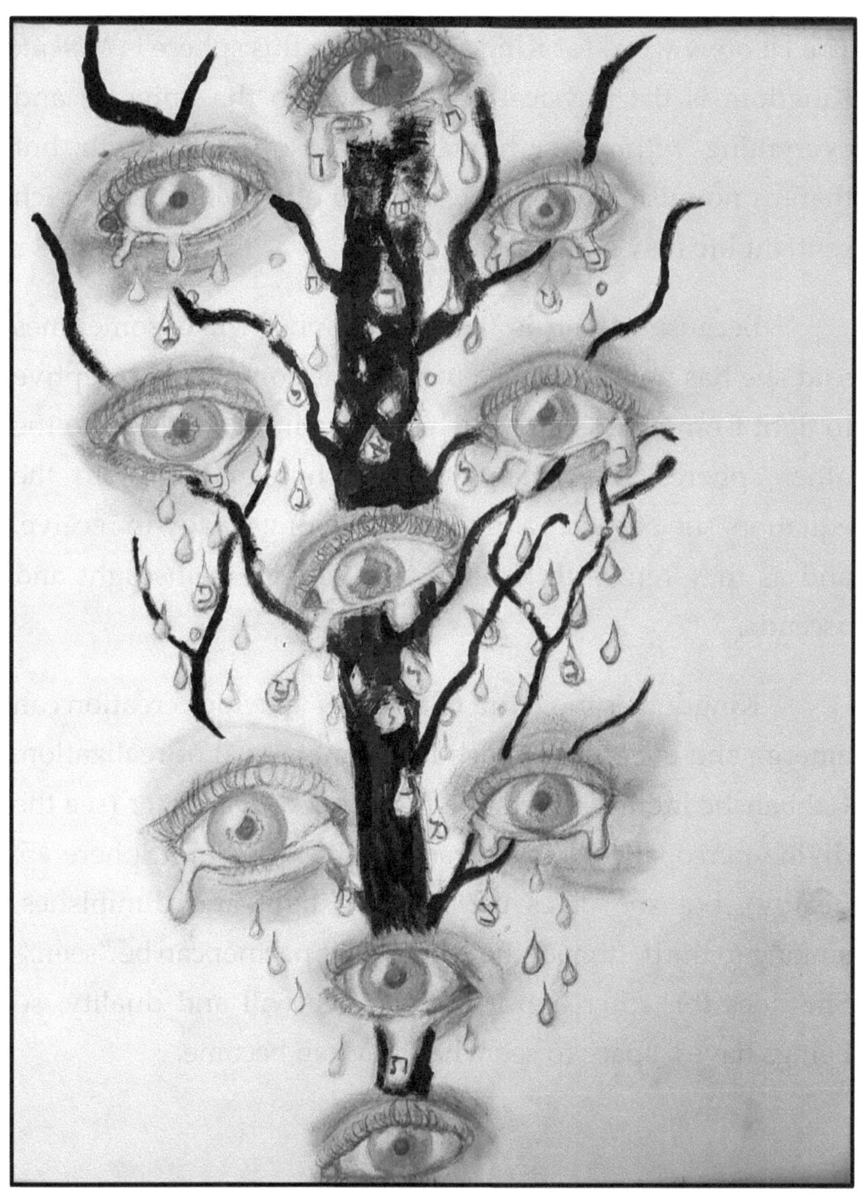

Sphere 1: Kingdom

The first sphere is called Kingdom and could rightfully be called Queendom because it embraces the Divine Feminine. The Hebrew word for Kingdom and for this sphere is *Malkut*. Kingdom is the physical creation within the universe and everything within. For humans this also means Earth, but there is no mistaking Sphere 1 is also other worlds in which sentient life may exist.

Because *Malkut* is the lowest sphere, it is sometimes said she has no light of her own and is completely receptive to light from other sources. This is true in relationship to the other spheres, but when you add human beings to the equation, she becomes a giver to any beings ready to receive, and as they return to their true selves, she gains light and ascends.

Kingdom is the "fruit of the tree," at which creation can emerge and eventually reach its ultimate goal of realization. Kabbalistic literature says the Kingdom as Daughter (see the divine personality below) was equal to the Son (Sphere #5: Beauty), but she gives up her own light and diminishes, sinking to the bottom of the Tree, so her partner can be "seen." She does this to create a place of free will and duality, so beings have a space to see what they can become.

The *Qlipah* analog to *Malkut* is named Lilith. This sphere represents physical creation but in its more violent aspects. As a *Qlipah* it represents tsunamis, earthquakes, and the hunter eating prey - all the violent and destructive forces of creation. Many Kabbalists say the world is a play of beauty and horror, life and death. *Malkut* is life. while the sphere of Lilith is death. Both are beautiful and yet both are horrific.

Hebrew Name: *Malkut* (Kingdom)

Location: Bottom of Central Pillar (Compassion)

Hebrew Divine Name: *Adonai* (Lord) or *Shekinah* (God's female presence and power)

Personality: The Daughter (*Nukvah*) or Bride (*Kallah*)

Qlipoth: Lilith (Queen of the Night)

Qlipoth Entity: Na'amah

Aspect of Lilith: Na'amah and Qarinah

Deities: Pan, Ceres, Demeter, Geb, Marduk, Nisaba, Cernnunnos, Myrddin

Archangel: Sandalfon

Order of Angels: *Ashim*

Astrological Attribute: The Earth

Level of the Soul: Bestial Soul (*Nefesh Behomet*)

Chakra: Root

Meditation: Mudra (physical movement as meditation)

Ritual Topic: The Pentacle

Holy Day: Yule

Color: Multi-colored, Earth Tones

Incense/Plant: Dittany of Crete, Lily, Carnation, Ivy, Narcissus

Adonai

In Hebrew, the Divine name of Kingdom is *Adonai* which means "Lord." This has been associated with the male form of deity, but it is really referencing deity around us and seemingly separated from us. In Kabbalah anything which gives is male and everything which receives is female. This is not pointing to a difference in male and female humans – we are all a mixture of the male and female energy of giving and receiving. However, the name of "God" at Kingdom is called "Lord" to show an external aspect giving to us. In Hebrew, another divine name at this Sphere is *Shekinah* which means

"God's presence and power." *Shekinah* is perceived as female and seen as the Daughter and Mother aspect of divinity.

Daughter and Bride

Malkut is the realm of the Daughter and Bride. She is a representation of all beings who are god/dess's child, but specifically, when we choose to reunite with our true self, we become the Bride. Deities associated with this sphere can be male or female because the Daughter and Bride are archetypes rather than gender. At the heart of Kabbalah, all sentient beings can become the divine personality of the Bride once they consciously choose reunification and are able to embody it.

One of the primary names of God in Hebrew is *Yahweh*. *Yahweh*, meaning "who was, is, and will be," is made up of four Hebrew letters: *Yod, Heh, Vav, Heh*. These four letters represent the four primary personalities of God within Kabbalah. *Yod* represents Father (*Abba*); the first *Heh* represents Mother (*Aima*); the *Vav* represents Son (*Ben*); and the final *Heh* represents Daughter (*Nukvah*) and Bride (*Kallah*). The most sacred name of God also represents all divinity in all his/her aspects in relationship. The fact both the Mother and the Daughter/Bride are represented by the same Hebrew letter (*Heh*) points to them being Intrinsically related. The

Mother is *Shekinah* or Holy Spirit outside of creation, while the Bride is *Shekinah* or Holy Spirit inside creation. Any sentient being can evolve from Daughter to Bride as creation becomes increasingly conscious and divine, as beings transform into who they really are.

Na'amah

Na'amah (meaning "pleasant") is closely related to Lilith in Jewish tradition. In some stories she is Lilith's sister and in others her daughter. The name Na'amah is mentioned in Genesis 4:22 as a descendant of Cain. She was the only mentioned daughter of Lamech and Zillah, and their youngest named child. Her brother was Tubal-Cain, while Jabal and Jubal were her half-brothers, sons of Lamech's other wife, Adah. In *Midrash*, Noah's wife is named Na'amah. She is also mentioned as Noah's wife in the Quran, and it calls her an "evil woman."

In Jewish legend, Na'amah is said to be similar to Lilith. She, too, is called a consort of Samael, and mates with Adam after his fall from the Garden. She is identified with one of the women who cause the Watchers to sin and become fallen angels. Na'amah preys on weak men and uses them for her own ends, making her an archetypical seductress. She is described as incredibly beautiful, but very wrathful.

Na'amah is mentioned in *Zohar* and *Midrash* several times, but usually in conjunction with Lilith. There are a few references to her individually; for example: "And these two Creator-appointed rulers swim in the Great Sea, fly up from there, and at night go to Na'amah, the mother of witches, for whom the first people fell."

In Kabbalah, Na'amah is associated with the physical world and the *Qlipah* (husk of darkness) named Lilith. Na'amah, being a human woman according to scriptures, is a physical incarnation of Lilith and her aspect in the world. The above quotation from *Zohar* indicates her role as the progenitor of witches, who are also incarnate beings. This contrasts with Lilith, whose children the Lilin are non-corporeal beings of spirit.

Through the concept of *Partzufim* (divine personalities), Na'amah and Lilith can be considered separate beings with their own personalities and attributes. However, they are really the same consciousness at different levels of creation. This does not preclude a practitioner from working with either Na'amah or Lilith or both, but it is important to remember that their base energy comes from the same source.

Qarinah

In Arabic mythology there is a Jinn name Qarinah also called "the Mother of Children" who was rejected by Adam and mated with *Iblis* (a fallen angel). Her story sounds very similar to that of Lilith as she is said to give birth to many demon children and to take revenge on Adam, she kills human children, and makes men impotent.

Sandalfon

The Archangel Sandalfon is called the "Shoe Angel" and is said to walk the earth. Sandalfon is the angel of Mother God, who walks with all beings who know her. Sandalfon's purpose is to join physical reality to the Endless Light (*Ain Sof Or*) beyond creation. In *Midrash,* Sandalfon is the twin sister of Metatron, the supernal Archangel of Sphere 10: Crown. In actuality, Sandalfon and Metatron are at their core the same being. Sphere 1: Kingdom and Sphere 10: Crown are linked. In Kabbalah, it is often said, "*Malkut* (Sphere 1) is in *Keter* (Sphere 10) and *Keter* (Sphere 10) is in *Malkut* (Sphere 1)." The Divine Light is at the core of creation which in its primordial state, is at the heart of the supernal realm.

The *Ashim*

The *Ashim* are an order of angels called "souls of fire." Some of them are tiny and control things like gravity, the strong/weak nuclear forces, and anything which keeps matter held together. In addition, the *Ashim* also look after evolution, birth and death, and are associated with every group of people.

Nefesh (earthly soul)

Nefesh is the ego and personality, often called "the flesh" in Christian scripture. This part of the soul burns off at death and usually disintegrates, although in some cases it becomes earth bound and becomes a "ghost." There are two forms of the *Nefesh– Nefesh Behomet* (bestial soul focused on ego) and *Nefesh Elokit* (enlightened soul focused on our true self).

Root Chakra (located at the base of the spine)

Located at the base of the spine, the root chakra corresponds to our physical or material body and life in this world, and with all our basic needs for survival. This chakra also encompasses the energy of the matter composing our bodies and the world; the need for food, shelter, and clothing; the instinct for survival and procreation; the ability to ground ourselves spiritually and emotionally; and intelligence of the physical body. The earth and the direction are also attributes of the root chakra.

The body we inhabit is tied directly to the material world and our manifestation in it. Although we may speak of our body as separate from our soul/spirit, in truth they are linked and necessary for incarnation. Basically, our physical body is an interface between our soul and the world around us; higher vibrations of energy inhabiting a physical form.

Mudra

Meditation is an important part of any spiritual practice. For Sphere #1 we will focus on Mudra, which is a type of physical meditation involving moving of the body. Other examples of physical meditation are yoga and martial arts.

The following Mudra can be practiced when you want to encourage energy from above to come into the physical plane:

- Place your hands above your head, placing your left hand over the right.
- Breathe in.

- Keep your hands in the same position but lower them down so your arms are pointing down with your hands in the same position.
- Exhale.
- Perform this moving meditation several times and focus on the idea of "As Above, So Below."

Pentacle

Ritual items can be acquired as part of the process of working with the spheres. If you do not have money to purchase items, you can make do with what you have. For instance, a piece of paper cut into a circular shape or a relatively flat, round stone can be used as a pentacle. Going on a quest for spiritual items is a meditative and magickal practice of its own. You can also begin with "starter" ritual items which you intend to replace over time which resonate better with your practice.

The pentacle can be a traditional pentagram, or it can be any disc-shaped object. It is whatever you are more comfortable using. Pentacles are typically made of wood, stone, or crystal, but symbolically anything which is flat, and circular can be used. This tool is used in ritual and meditation to represent the element of Earth. As stated earlier in this section, Sphere 1 is about the physical universe and the earth, so this ritual tool is aptly paired to Kingdom. The pentacle is seen as a severe element (meaning it is restrictive) and an extremely physical one. When using object in any spiritual movement. it can represent Kingdom (Sphere 1), Earth, pillar of Mercy on the Tree, and any physical manifestation.

Yule (Winter Solstice)

Yule is the shortest day of the year, the day with the most restriction of light, and thus it is of the Kingdom–our world. It is the day of death and of rebirth, and the beginning of cycles. Many celebrate this day by praying for the return of the sun and the light, seeking renewal. This feast day is also associated with "apocalypse," meaning "revelation." The revelation of Yule is so profound it feels like the end, but it is a new beginning. The purpose of this festival from a Gnostic Kabbalah point of view, is to revere the earth and physical incarnation.

Sphere 2: Foundation

This sphere is called Foundation (*Yesod*) and is the conduit through which energy passes between sphere 1 and the rest of the Tree. Conversely, it is also the conduit through which the energy of all three pillars combines and flow down into Kingdom (*Malkut*). Merciful, severe, and compassionate energy flows down from above, through *Yesod* and into the last sphere (*Malkut*), the fruit of the Tree. The proportional mix of this energy is determined by the thoughts and desires of humanity, drawing the energy down.

Consciousness then flows back up the tree through Foundation, and all the way up to the highest spheres. This is the path of the soul, and the path of prayers as they rise back up to the source of all creation. If we use the middle pillar meditation (a Kabbalistic practice), our goal is to raise our consciousness up the Tree through the middle pillar and then bring back what experiences we can embody as thought in our brain and mind.

The *Qlipah* associated with the sphere of Foundation is *Gamaliel. Gamaliel (The Obscene Ones)* is the shadow of the "world soul" and associated with dreams, nightmares, and astral travel. Because this sphere is a shadow, it represents the dreams mankind does not wish to acknowledge, the desires which are forbidden, and unbridled sexuality. These, of course, are all things everyone needs to confront on their path to enlightenment, but they are contained in a place in which many get stuck, unable to traverse such a psychic expanse. The emotions and desires fulfilled in *Gamaliel* are not "evil," but when hidden and denied they can take dangerous turns.

Hebrew Name: *Yesod* (Foundation)

Location: Second from Bottom of Central Pillar (Compassion)

Hebrew Divine Name: *Shaddai* (Almighty), *El Shaddai* (Almighty God), and *Shaddai El Chai* (Almighty Living God)

Personality: Teacher and healer

Qlipoth: *Gamaliel* (The Obscene Ones)

Qlipoth Entity: Lilith

Aspect of Lilith: Lilith the Younger and *Pomba Gira* (the *Lilin*)

Deities: Goda, Diana, Thoth, Ganesha, Sin, Myestats, Soma

Archangel: Gabriel

Order of Angels: *Kerubim*

Astrological Attribute: The Moon

Level of the Soul: Heavenly Soul (*Nefesh Elokit)*

Chakra: Navel

Meditation: Ecstatic Worship

Ritual Topic: Cup or Chalice

Holy Day: Imbolc

Color: Purple

Incense/Plant: Jasmine, Comfrey, Camphor, Aloes

Shaddai, El Shaddai, and *Shaddai El Chai*

Sphere 2 has three divine names: *Shaddai, El Shaddai,* and *Shaddai El Chai*. These names mean Almighty, Almighty God, and Almighty Living God. There are three divine names because all energy from above flows through Foundation into Kingdom in the form of mercy, severity, and compassion.

Yesod and the name *Shaddai* are often associated with the phallus because *Yesod* is the sphere which connects the upper tree with *Malkut,* and thus sexual imagery is often used. However, another interpretation of *Shaddai* is the "breasted one" and refers to God as Mother.

Teacher and Healer

Sphere 2 is the realm of the teacher or healer. In Jewish tradition, the personality of Foundation is the righteous one (*Tzaddik*), one who is on a path of enlightenment. For our purposes we will use the teacher and healer archetypes as the personality of the sphere. He or she is both external and the part of us which understands our connection to all. Deities of this sphere are often associated with love and sexuality because of their dual natures, giving and receiving. The myth cycles portray this sphere as the place of sexual union between the Bride (at *Malkut*) and the upper realms.

Lilith the Succubus

At this sphere in the Tree of Shadows, it is all aspects of Lilith but especially her guise as a succubus and seducer. She is the demoness in Jewish lore who comes to men sleeping alone and causes them to have lurid dreams producing nocturnal emissions. Lilith is then said to take this creative energy to birth demonic children with it.

Part of the sexualization of Lilith came about because of the lore saying she left Adam, becoming the first divorced woman. In the Middle Ages and especially in Jewish culture at that time, a divorced woman was often seen as promiscuous and seductive, always looking for a new husband. Lilith is sensual and a being free of the restraints of society, but she is not a being who "needs a man" to complete her.

Lilith The Younger

Kabbalistic texts often refer to two Liliths. The first, Lilith the Elder, is the being who is called "the first wife of Adam." She is the one created in Genesis 1, whose masculine side is Samael. Lilith the Younger is said to be the daughter of *Qaftzefoni,* the Prince and King of Heaven, and his wife *Mehetrebel,* the daughter of *Matred.* Little is documented in Jewish lore about this mysterious couple, but their daughter, Lilith the Younger, was married to Ashmedai (Asmodeus). Ashmedai is the king of the *shedim* (demons composed of human souls which have never had bodies).

Later texts claim Lilith the Younger battled against Lilith the Elder. Beyond these few Kabbalistic stories, it is unclear how Lilith the Elder, and Lilith the Younger differ, which one is being referenced in *Midrash* and other extra-Biblical texts, and why there is conflict between the two, other than jealousy.

It is conceivable this myth is a representation of the battle between the redeemed and unredeemed Lilith–the part of her who has found enlightenment and the part who is still existing in separation. Which Lilith is the "redeemed" one is up for interpretation depending on the story. Lilith the Elder is a primordial being who eventually finds enlightenment, although at many times in her long history she is far from pure. Lilith the Younger is said to be the child of heavenly beings, but is married to Ashmedai, who is a being of admixture. A case can be made for either to be the more "righteous" in any situation. Unfortunately, the *Midrash* never clarifies this point, so we are left to debate it on our own.

Pomba Gira / Lilin

The Jewish *Midrash* and other Kabbalistic works all talk about Lilith giving birth to a legion of demon children. These children are from various fathers, including Samael, Ashmedai, Adam (while he is separated from Eve), and all the men Lilith has seduced into nocturnal emissions. Not much is said about these beings, but they are mentioned in various texts as *Lilin*, *Lilu*, Succubae, Incubi, night demons, and wind spirits. The *Lilin* and Succubae are female, while the *Lilu* and Incubi are male. The terms night demons and wind spirits are most frequently used to refer to these beings collectively.

Succubus and Incubus have popped up repeatedly in myth and legend, but relatively few mentions are made of the *Lilin* and *Lilu*.

In *Embracing Lilith,* I have a section which discusses the *Pomba Gira* from the Afro-Brazilian Tradition of *Quimbonda.* In this book I want to explore the teachings of *Quimbonda* in more detail, because I think this is where the best information on the *Lilin* and *Lilu* can be found. It is important to point out I am not an initiate of *Quimbonda,* and anything I discuss on this topic is from my study of the subject and my working with the spirits in my own paradigm. So, nothing in this section should be misconstrued as official teachings of *Quimbonda.*

Quimbonda is a tradition which evolved in Brazil, bringing together teachings from the native Brazilian culture and spiritual ideas imported by African slaves. Because Brazil was a place of exile for many occultists as well, Kabbalah and ritual magic are also intertwined in the *Quimbonda* system. The Catholic Church deems *Quimbonda* heretical and calls it Satanic. Unlike many of the other South American spiritual traditions which used the Church to hide their religion (such as *Santeria*), *Quimbonda* practitioners decided to embrace the Satanic paradigm calling their practice black magic.

At the center of *Quimbonda* are two types of spirit. The first is the *Exu* – a legion of fierce male spirits ruling over the various kingdoms of the world. The name *Exu* may have originated from the Yoruba Trickster God, *Eshu*; however, some have theorized *Exu* comes from the Hebrew word *Exud* which means "traitor." These spirits can be spirits of the dead or pre-existing spirits of nature which have been syncretized into *Quimbonda*. The three Exu rulers are Satan (Samael), Beelzebub (Belial), and Asmodeus (Ashmedai), with all the other *Exu* falling under one of the three according to their type and Kingdom. The second type of spirit is the *Pomba Gira*–a legion of wild female spirits who also rule over the various kingdoms of the world. *Pomba Gira* means "turning Dove," alluding to the idea of the female Spirit (Dove), but one which is turning or spiraling in a chaotic fashion. The *Pomba Gira* are similar to the *Exu,* seen as either the spirits of the dead or pre-existing elemental spirits who have been absorbed into the *Pomba Gira* archetype. The queen of *Pomba Gira* is Lilith and their mother is Na'amah.

It is fascinating that the *Pomba Gira* are directly associated with Lilith and her more earthly manifestation, Na'amah. In parallel, the *Exu* are associated with the arch demons who most often appear as consorts of Lilith, Na'amah, and Agrat. The teachings and legends about *Exu* and *Pomba Gira* show them to be remarkably similar in nature to Lilith. They are called demons, but at the same time invoked for protection, assistance, and advice. Some practitioners of *Quimbonda* state the *Exu* and *Pomba Gira* are agents of human spiritual evolution. My study and practice bring me to the idea the *Exu* and *Pomba Gira* are Lilith's children. The *Exu* are the *Lilu,* her children with her demon consorts, who took on the appearance and attributes of their fathers. The *Pomba Gira* are the *Lilin,* her children from the seed of men which Lilith steals, creating spirits in her image and nature. Both the *Exu* and *Pomba Gira* can also be the spirits of dead humans who have been transformed by suffering and desire. These are still Lilith's spiritual children even if they were not birthed by her directly.

Every *Exu* and *Pomba Gira* belong to one of the nine Kingdoms. These kingdoms are rough categorizations of the energy the spirit works with. It is important to note that there are unlimited numbers of both *Exu* and *Pomba Gira,* which means one person may have one kind of experience with a guide from a certain Kingdom, and someone else may have a quite different experience with another guide from the same kingdom.

The Nine Kingdoms are:

- Kingdom of the Cemetery (*Cemiterio*)
    - Knowledge of the dead
- Kingdom of the Crossroads (*Encruzilhadas*)
    - Knowledge of places of power

- Kingdom of the Sepulchers (*Catacombs*)
    - Knowledge of the dark
- Kingdom of the Lyre (*Lira*)
    - Knowledge of the arts
- Kingdom of the Streets (*Cigana*)
    - Knowledge of life
- Kingdom of the Wilderness (*Mata*)
    - Knowledge of nature
- Kingdom of the Soul (*Alma*)
    - Knowledge of souls
- Kingdom of the Ocean Shore (*Praia*)
    - Knowledge of waves and wind (the heart)
- Kingdom of the Ocean (*Calunga*)
    - Knowledge of tide and moon (absence)

Gabriel

The Archangel Gabriel, The Strength of God, is the being who presides over divine messages. Since Gabriel is located at Sphere 2, this is where all messages from deity flow into creation. Gabriel usually manifests in a more feminine form and is associated with the color blue, water, and the West. West is the door of death, so Gabriel is also associated with death, dying, and the transition between worlds. Archangels can be helpful on the spiritual path, but they can also be frightening beings of severity. Some legends depict Gabriel transforming into a dragon and destroying anything in her way. Gabriel is the archangel who guards *Tebel-Vilon,* the first heaven, a spiritual paradise which has every plant and animal which has ever existed on earth. This is where the garden of Eden is located.

The *Kerubim*

It is not surprising that the *Kerubim,* the order of angels overseeing Foundation, are doorways because *Yesod* is considered a gateway. *Kerubim* are associated with any doorway, including physical doors within buildings and portals to other dimensions. They control the flow of energy in both directions and are the guardians who ensure that none pass who are not ready for the journey. Because *Kerubim* are described as "little faces," they were eventually synchrotized with the god Cupid and are now frequently pictured as winged babies called cherubs.

Nefesh Elokit

Nefesh Elokit is the ego or personality, but when it aspires upward and toward the soul's true self it becomes "heavenly." In this state we are aware of our unity with all creation, and we begin to search for what is beyond the physical. The soul is not static, so as humans we often flicker between *Nefesh Elokit* and *Nefesh Behomet* (the bestial personality). Awakening *Nefesh Elokit* is the beginning of enlightenment.

Navel Chakra (Located in the stomach)

The navel chakra corresponds to our astral body, to astral worlds, and to dreams. Associated with emotions, pleasure and sexuality, movement, change and polarity, this chakra encompasses the play of duality and opposition necessary for individuation and self-realization, socialization and exchanges of energy, nourishment, and nurturance. The navel chakra connects to the elemental force of water and the direction West. It is also the dynamic center of life and vital energy, which when joined to the heart becomes the vehicle of self-realization. When joined to the heart, the navel or belly becomes like a womb through which we conceive, gestate, and give birth to something of our true being, our enlightened soul. Yet when divorced from the intelligence of the heart it is the "belly of the beast," a source of extreme selfishness, ego, fear, which can be bound up in self-destruction.

Ecstatic Worship

For Sphere 2 we will focus on ecstatic worship. This type of mediation involves losing oneself to Spirit.

Ecstatic worship is the process of letting one's mind merge into deity. This can be done through music, dance, chanting, or other methods. The idea is to enter a place of praise for the deity and then let go of consciousness by focusing on whatever activity we have chosen to take us out of ourselves. Many will sing or dance, but other forms of worship such as chanting or even painting can be used.

- Turn on music.
- Release yourself into a place of praise.
- Focus on a spirit of thankfulness.
- Sing, move, whatever you are called to do.
- When you feel you are done, turn off the music and reflect on your experience.

Cup or Chalice

If you do not have money to purchase items, you can make do with what you have. For instance, you can find a suitable cup in your kitchen cabinet.

The cup can be a traditional chalice, or it can be a *Kapala* (Buddhist skull cup). It should be whatever you are most comfortable using. Ritual chalices are typically made of metal, wood, stone, crystal, or bone, but symbolically anything which can hold liquid can be used. The chalice is a merciful (expansive) ritual tool and is the container of spirit (water or other liquid) that represents the doorway of *Yesod*.

Imbolc (Middle of Winter)

Like Yule, Imbolc is also held during the winter months, but celebrates the lengthening days and the hope and promise of Spring to come. It marks a transition period between Winter's desolation and the rebirth of Spring. For this holiday we call for new life and renewal. From a Gnostic Kabbalah point of view, the festival focuses on foundation, the link to spirit, and the movement up and down the tree.

Sphere 3: Splendor

This Sphere is called Splendor (*Hod*) and is associated with the Mage or Magician. It is also called "the hazy mirror of prophecy," meaning it is also associated with prophetic movements, but those in which the messages are hazy, confusing, and not as sure to transpire. Also representing the intellect (thoughts) and upper astral, Splendor is the first Sphere on the pillar of severity (restriction). The previous two spheres discussed are in the middle of the tree and help form the pillar of compassion. Severity is not evil or even bad; it is the pull of energy which drives evolution.

The corresponding *Qlipah* is called Samael. Samael is the male counterpart to Lilith and is associated with dark intellect. His name means "Poison of God" because he is the poison which draws beings away from their enlightenment by tempting them back into their ego. This may sound evil, but it is not. He draws the ego into full bloom showing consciousness egoism is not the answer and thus enlightenment dawns. Mastering consciousness of the *Qlipah* Samael will bring about mastery of the serpent energy of Kundalini. The poison becomes the antidote.

Hebrew Name: *Hod* (Splendor)

Location: Bottom of Left Pillar (Severity)

Hebrew Divine Name: *Elohim Tzavaot* (Gods of Creation)

Personality: The Magician

Qlipoth: Samael (The Poison of God)

Qlipoth Entity: Adramelech

Aspect of Lilith: Az (Lilit) and Qualilitu

Deities: Thoth, Hermes, Mercury, Anubis, Ogma

Archangel: Michael

Order of Angels: *Beni Elohim*

Astrological Attribute: Mercury

Level of the Soul: Spirit (Lower *Ruach)*

Chakra: Solar Plexus

Meditation: Primordial Meditation

Ritual Topic: the Wand

Holy Day: Ostara

Color: Orange

Incense/Plant: Storax, Orchid, Peyote

Elohim Tzavaot

Elohim is a Hebrew word composed of a masculine singular noun (*El*) which means "god," and a plural feminine modifier (ohim). This name is sometimes translated as "gods and goddesses," but because Judaism is monotheistic, the more proper translation is probably "one god with multiple male and female personalities." Even though *Elohim* has both a masculine and feminine component, in Kabbalah it is often associated with the Divine Feminine. The full name of *Elohim Tzavaot* is translated as "God of Hosts." Another way to think of this name is to consider it "gods and goddesses of creation," including both physical and spiritual manifestation.

Mage or Magician

The third sphere is the realm of the mage or magician. He or she is the representation of those who can perform magic both internal and external to themselves. All practitioners embody the magician, and all are the instrument of transformation.

Adramelech

Adramelech is called the peacock demon. The imagery of peacock feathers shows the nature of Adramelech as he rules over individuality, beauty, and is all-seeing. He helps the Magician to break free from the expectations of society hindering them from mastering magic. Together, Adramelech and the Magician work to replace societal norms and inhibitions with impulses that create true beauty.

Az (Lilit)

In *Zoroastrianism,* Az is the demon of avarice, gluttony, insatiability, and lust. Az is often paired with Niyaz (want) and is featured also in *Zurvanite* and *Manichaean* texts. In one text, Az swallows everything and anything to satisfy her want, but she is never fulfilled.

In Manichaeism, Az is a female demon who is the mother of all demons and sin. She formed the human body and imprisoned the soul in it. She is physical matter which leads to evil, and tries to make humanity forget its divine origins, thus preventing people from finding their enlightenment.

In Gnostic Kabbalah, Az (also called Lilit) is the aspect of Lilith who is anthropomorphized as part human and part animal. Her most common forms are that of the spider goddess (human upper half and spider bottom half) or as a lamia (human upper half and snake bottom half). However, she can appear in many forms and many animal-human hybrid manifestations.

In the guise of the spider goddess, Az is able to traverse the Tree of Life and the Tree of Shadows by moving between *Sephirot* and *Qlipoth,* using them as doorways. The Trees are her web, and she stalks her pray along the pathways, searching for travelers. If the practitioner can see beyond fear and duality, she will help them on their journey, if not, she will turn them back in terror.

Qualilitu

Qualilitu is the aspect of Lilith as a mermaid. She is half woman and half fish (as are most depictions of mermaids). Qualilitu swims through consciousness diving deep into our souls to adapt our being toward greater depths of understanding and transformation. In Quimbonda, the *Pomba Gira* Poquina has all the same attributes and intentions as Qualilitu. As queen of the sea (being the great graveyard),

Poquina ferries souls who have died unjustly through the waters of consciousness.

Michael

The archangel Michael, "Who is Like Unto God," is said to be a warrior and protector. He brings peace but will fight when necessary. Michael is associated with the color red, fire, and South. He is typically portrayed as a masculine figure in red armor, wielding a sword and sometimes bearing a shield. He can be called upon for protection or in conjunction with Lilith. Call upon Michael and picture yourself bathed in a shield of red light.

Beni Elohim

The order of angels called the *Beni Elohim* are the most skilled at interacting with physical incarnation. *Beni Elohim* means "sons of God," and these angels are said to be able to easily possess human beings if allowed. The movie *Fallen* with Denzel Washington is about a demon of the order *Beni Elohim*. The *Beni Elohim* are also the famed Watchers who fell because of their attraction to and seduction of human women (in some lore the main seductress is Na'amah).

Spirit (Lower *Ruach*)

The *Ruach* is composed of both the human intelligence and the divine intelligence. The lower *Ruach* points toward the *Nefesh* (earthly soul) and is our intelligence, while the upper *Ruach* points toward the *Neshamah* (eternal soul) and toward enlightenment.

Solar Plexus Chakra (located between stomach and heart)

The solar plexus chakra corresponds with our mental body and the mental world, the ordinary mind or surface consciousness, the force of personal will or power, the transformation and delivery of energy, the knowledge and ability necessary for works of magick, all intellectual pursuits, technology, and humor. It also corresponds to the elemental force of fire and the direction South.

When the solar plexus is joined to the heart, the mental consciousness becomes illuminated and inspired. The solar plexus then acts as the receiver and transmitter of spiritual energy from above. With this joining all human endeavors assume their true purpose and meaning, generating a true humanity in balance with the All. However, when cut off from the heart, this chakra is the "head of the beast," and the life is bound up in the power of egotism, or power over others. Selfish ambition potentially knows no satisfaction.

Religions preaching a revelation of love but enacting holy wars and inquisitions are an example of the resulting darkness of this center when divorced from the heart and upper chakras.

Primordial Meditation

For Sphere 3 we will focus on the beginnings of mindfulness training.

Primordial meditation is the type of meditation present in many traditions as the basis for all mindfulness training. The purpose of primordial meditation is to clear the mind, learn to manage thoughts and emotions, and listen.

- Get into a comfortable position.
- Push all thoughts aside and begin to breath in a regular rhythm.
- Breathe in… and out… in… and out.
- As thoughts arise, gently push them aside and refocus on your breathing.

It is important not to get upset or agitated over thoughts which arise. Our minds are noisy, and it takes time and practice to reach longer periods of silent mind.

Start with a short session. It is much more important to have consistent practice than to have long practice and you can always increase your meditation length over time. If you have trouble not thinking about time, you can set a timer at the start of your practice. Begin with a short period like five minutes.

Wand

If you do not have money to purchase items, you can make do with what you have. For instance, a wand can be made by simply going outside and picking up a small branch.

The wand can be a traditional wooden rod, or it can be made from wood, stone, bone, or crystal. It should be made of whatever you are more comfortable using. The wand is a pointer that is associated with mercy (expansiveness), the element of fire (although some traditions associate it with air instead), and focuses energy in a particular direction. The simplest form of this magick tool is a stick.

Ostara (Spring Equinox)

Ostara marks the time when the sun passes over the celestial equator. It is a festival that celebrates the seasons' change from dark winter to brightening spring and full regeneration. The purpose of Ostara from a Gnostic Kabbalah point of view is to focus on magick and the power of spirit.

Sphere 4: Victory

The fourth Sphere is called Victory (*Netzach*), and it is associated with the Prophet and Prophecy. This Sphere is also called "the clear mirror of prophecy," meaning it is associated with prophetic movements which are clear and certain. *Netzach* can be seen in our consciousness as the generation of emotions and instincts. It is the interface between our mind, soul, and emotions.

The *Qlipoth* of *A'arab Zaraq*, the Ravens of Dispersion, is the dark side of Victory. This sphere is battle and holds all the forces the mage needs to win the war for self-transformation. The dove is often a sign of peace and of hope. *A'arab Zaraq* is associated with ravens which are associated with war and forbidden wisdom. Several dark deities of war have the raven as their symbol, including the Celtic *Morrigan*. The raven of *A'arab Zaraq* is the soul of the practitioner who must traverse unwanted dark emotions to take them through the dark night of the soul.

Hebrew Name: *Netzach* (Victory)

Location: Bottom of Right Pillar (Mercy)

Hebrew Divine Name: *Yahweh Tzavaot* (Lord God of Creation)

Personality: The Prophet

Qlipoth: *A'arab Zaraq* (The Ravens of Dispersion)

Qlipoth Entity: *Baal*

Aspect of Lilith: Ardat Lili (Lilitu)

Deities: Venus, Ishtar, Aphrodite, Hathor, Rhiannon, Niamh, Olwen

Archangel: Uriel

Order of Angels: The *Elohim*

Astrological Attribute: Venus

Level of the Soul: Spirit (Upper Ruach)

Chakra: Heart

Meditation: Primordial Meditation With an object

Ritual Topic: Knife or Athame

Holy Day: Beltane

Color: Green

Incense/Plant: Rose, Laurel, Red Sandalwood

Yahweh Tzavaot

Yahweh is composed of four Hebrew letters--*Yod Heh Vav Heh* and is known as the Tetragrammaton. In Judaism this is the most holy name of God. The Hebrew scriptures, also known as the Christian Old Testament, were originally written in Hebrew but then translated to Latin, and then English. There are several varying transliterations of the Hebrew names because of the different Alphabets. The name *Jehovah* is the same name as *Yahweh* but taken from the Latin spelling of the name rather than the Hebrew.

Y*ahweh* means "He who was, is, and shall be"; however, in Kabbalah the name also represents four major personalities of deity –Father (*Yod*), Mother (*Heh*), Son (*Vav*), and Daughter (final *Heh*). Even though *Yahweh* has masculine and feminine components in the individual letters, *Yahweh* is most often seen as male. The full name of *Yahweh Tzavaot* is translated as "Lord of Hosts." Another way to think of this name is to consider it "Lord God of Creation," including both physical and spiritual manifestation.

The Prophet

Netzach is the realm of the prophet. He or She is the representation of those who receive divine messages. In

Hebrew, the word for prophet is *Navi*. This is not necessarily someone who gets premonitions of what is to come, but instead one who gets spiritual messages for themselves and others. These messages come from the higher realms of the Tree as energy flows down into *Netzach*.

Baal

Baal was originally a Canaanite deity of storms whose name simply means Lord. In Canaanite mythology, Baal was the primary god with *Yahweh* serving as a lesser deity. Eventually certain Semitic peoples, later named Israelites, made *Yahweh* their primary deity and Baal was demonized. In grimoires of the Middle Ages, Baal is renamed Bael and included as one of the seven princes of Hell.

Baal is said to be a demon who can make a favored practitioner invisible, and he can transmit great knowledge. His dominions seem to be knowledge, power, and love. He can appear as a great king, a cat, or a toad. His original appearance as a deity was as a horned king.

Ardat Lili **(Lilitu)**

Ardat Lili first appears as a Sumerian storm spirit, predating the mention of Lilith or Lilitu in myth and legend. She is later considered a succubus and vampire who seduces men into masturbation. She is also said to marry men to create havoc in their lives.

Even though Ardat Lili's name is listed prior to Lilith in written record, later demonic tradition calls her Lilith's first-born daughter with Samael. I consider her an aspect of Lilith because she shares all the same attributes and basic Sumerian origins. Ardat Lili is primarily mentioned in the early Sumerian period, while the name Lilitu appears later in the Akkadian and Babylonian periods.

Uriel

The Archangel Uriel is an angel of magick and ritual. Uriel helps us to manifest magick and energy in the world. She most often appears in a female form. Uriel, the archangel of miracles, is useful to call on as a help in any magickal action. She is associated with the color green, the Earth, and North.

The *Elohim*

The word *Elohim* is usually translated from Hebrew as one God who manifests as many gods and goddesses. When e*lohim* is not capitalized, it refers to the order of angels of the same name, which includes dominions, authorities, and principalities. These are the angels who watch over countries, groups, and organizations. It is also important to recognize that every order of angels also has a corresponding order of demons and of archons (dark and admixed forces).

Spirit (Upper *Ruach*)

The *Ruach* or Spirit is the human intelligence and the divine intelligence. The upper *Ruach* points toward the *Neshamah* (eternal soul) and toward enlightenment. When this upper level is engaged, our *Ruach* (or intelligence) is driven by our true self and less susceptible to the whims of the ego.

Heart Chakra (located behind the heart)

The heart chakra corresponds with our higher astral body and the higher worlds, and it corresponds with our true intelligence: faith, hope, love, and the understanding which come with them. This chakra is the seat of true spirituality. It is depth of feeling, active compassion, redemption, balance, and it corresponds with the elemental power of air and the direction East.

From the heart chakra, we recognize and realize our unity with all and begin to enter communion with divinity. Humankind struggles to come to the heart because it is here, we begin to become true human beings and begin to realize the divinity within us. The heart is the seat of enlightenment, our true self as we are in the Divine Mother. This is the place of true self-knowledge and specifically the knowledge of our purpose in this life. This chakra is the center of our true desires and dreams.

The heart chakra joins the three upper chakras with the three lower chakras, and thus this center is the key to the actualization of the full soul. Although we may incarnate in a human body, until we have realization in the heart, we are not yet a human being. This chakra is a principal center of the spirit present in material form.

Primordial Meditation With an Object

For Sphere 4 we will focus on another aspect of mindfulness training.

Primordial Meditation With breath is usually practiced with eyes closed, but you can also practice it with eyes open and focusing on an object instead of on your breathing.

Perform the primordial meditation as in Sphere 3 but keep your eyes open and focus on an object.

Examples of focal objects:

- Candle flame
- Statue
- Picture
- Or anything which holds significance to you

- Get into a comfortable position.
- Push all thoughts aside and begin to breathe in a regular rhythm.
- Breathe in… and out… in… and out.
- As thoughts arise, gently push them aside and re-focus on your breathing.
- Keep your vision focused on the item of your choice.
- It is important not to get upset or agitated over thoughts which arise. Our minds are noisy, and it takes time and practice to achieve longer periods of silent mind.

Start with a short session. It is much more important to have consistent practice than to have long practice and you can always increase your meditation length over time. If you have trouble not thinking about time, you can set a timer at the start of your practice. Begin with a short period like five minutes

Knife or Athame

If you do not have money to purchase items, you can make do with what you have. For instance, use a butter knife from your kitchen cabinet for this ritual tool. It does not have to be anything fancy.

The knife can be a traditional Athame, or it can be a *Phurba* (Buddhist 3-sided ritual knife). It can be made of what you are most comfortable using, typically metal or crystal, but symbolically anything with an edge can be used. This tool is associated with severity (restriction), air, and helps to "cut" symbolically.

Beltane (Height of Spring)

Beltane is the anglicized name for the Gaelic May Day festival. Most commonly it is held on May 1st, about halfway between the spring equinox and the summer solstice. Historically, it was widely observed throughout Ireland, Scotland and the Isle of Man and focused on fertility. The focus of this holiday from a Gnostic Kabbalah perspective is on prophecy and messages from deity.

Sphere 5: Beauty

This Sphere represents "Beauty" (*Tiferet*) and is the balancing agent between all things. This Sphere is associated with enlightened beings and all sacrificial gods because this is where we sacrifice our egoistic desires for those of the spiritual beings we truly are. In Jewish Kabbalah, *Tiferet* is the sphere of the messiah. Messiah means "anointed one" and does not have the connotation of "only begotten son of God" used by Christians. *Tiferet* is also the sphere of balance and enlightenment.

Thagirion in the Qlipah symbolizes dispute and the judicial process. The word Satan means "accuser" or "adversary" and is a title much like "lawyer." In Kabbalah there is not one Satan, because Satan is a position. Any being who works as an accuser is a Satan. *Tiferet* is associated with the son who is the bright Messiah, while *Thagirion* is associated with the son who is the dark Messiah or antichrist. Christianity teaches salvation through the Christ, while *Qlipothic* traditions teach salvation through oneself. In the end, the product is the same, enlightenment and finding our true self.

Hebrew Name: *Tiferet* (Beauty)

Location: Middle of the Central Pillar (Compassion)

Hebrew Divine Name: *Yaweh Elohenu* (Our Lord God)

Personality: The Messiah (anointed one)

Qlipoth: *Thagirion* (The Disputers)

Qlipoth Entity: Belphegor

Aspect of Lilith: Norea and Mary Magdalene

Deities: Osiris, Apollo, Attis, Adonis, Tammuz, Balder, Bran, Llew, Lugh, Yeshua, Dionysius, Bide, Nonens, Parva, Amaterasu, Ra

Archangel: Raphael

Order of Angels: *Malachim*

Astrological Attribute: The Sun

Level of the Soul: Heavenly Soul (*Neshama)*

Chakra: Throat

Meditation: Giving and Receiving

Ritual Topic: Crystal Ball

Holy Day: Litha (Summer Solstice)

Color: Gold/Yellow

Incense/Plant: Frankincense, Sunflower, Acacia, Buttercup, Chicory, Lovage, Marigold

Yahweh Elohenu

Yahweh Elohenu is another divine name composed of two portions. The first section is the same as in the last sphere, but the second portion is a cognate of Elohim (which we already saw two spheres ago). *Elohenu* is translated as "Our God" and refers to the idea of God being immanent. *Yahweh Elohenu* is then translated as "Our Lord God." It is associated with the idea of *Messiach* or Messiah in Hebrew Tradition. This is not the same as the Christian interpretation of Messiah, but instead a person who embodies the spirit of enlightenment.

Enlightened Ones

Tiferet is the realm of the enlightened ones. Enlightened ones are those who have transcended human consciousness through self-sacrifice and love. The is also the realm of the Divine Son who merges with the Bride in enlightenment. In Greek, some Gnostic traditions would call the Divine Son, *Logos* (Word) and the Divine Bride as *Sophia* (Wisdom).

Belphegor

Belphegor is the horned god of many religions in all his aspects as a solar and procreative deity. In the Judeo-Christian traditions he is one of the seven princes of hell, his name means "Lord of the Gap". He is a demon over discovery and creation of inventions. He is also known as the demon of sloth – one of the seven deadly sins. *Belphegor* originated as the Assyrian God, *Baal-Peor,* who was depicted as a phallus and associated with orgies.

Norea

Lilith is borrowed from Jewish *Midrash* by Gnostics, but generally the Gnostic female creative principle is called *Sophia,* Greek for "Wisdom." *Sophia* is both the bright and dark Mother, as well as Daughter or Bride, depending on the specific Gnostic text. At times she is portrayed as a great light working with the "unknowable" Father, and at other times she loses her light, falls into darkness, and creates hostile beings from the pain of her restriction in *Qlipoth.* In most of the Gnostic creation myths, *Sophia* creates the dark being known as *Demiurge* or *Yaldabaoth,* "False Creator." She later manifests as the serpent in the Garden of Eden. *Sophia* in Gnosticism is akin to *Shekinah* ("God's Presence and Power") in Kabbalah, but she is rarely given specific names to differentiate her bright and dark faces.

Two interesting exceptions are in the Gnostic texts "The Hypostasis of the Archons" and "The Thought of Norea." In both these writings, a female figure named Norea is central. Not mentioned anywhere else in Gnostic literature, little is known about her, but she is said to be either Eve's daughter or the wife of Noah. Interestingly, Norea is the Coptic/Greek version of the Hebrew name Na'amah and also means "pleasant." Midrash of Noah's wife being Na'amah was known and embraced by the later Gnostics. In "The Hypostasis of the Archons," Norea demands passage on the ark and when Noah denies her, she wields the power of fire and burns the entire ark to ash, leaving Noah to build a new one. Norea is seen as an enlightened Na'amah by Gnostics and is thus a perfect avatar for *Tiferet*.

Mary Magdalene

Mary Magdalene is only mentioned by name a few times in the New Testament, but her story has captured the minds and hearts of Gnostics. What is known about Magdalene from canonical scripture is that seven demons were supposedly cast from her, she is one of the few of *Yeshua's* (Jesus') followers that are at the cross during the Crucifixion, she assists in his burial, and she is the first to see him after he rises from the dead.

The Gnostic Gospels have many stories about Mary Magdalene. Almost all represent her as at the very least the most inner student of *Yeshua*. She understands his teachings and energetic transmissions when the male disciples do not. She is literally the "star" of these stories. To Gnostics Magdalene is seen as the embodiment of Mother and Daughter God and some traditions considered her to be the blending of both Lilith and Eve as a perfect enlightened being.

Raphael

The Archangel Raphael presides over knowledge and healing. He gives spiritual, mental, and physical healing to those who seek him. It is not a coincidence he manifests at *Tiferet*; this is because of its property of balance. Raphael (associated with the color yellow, air, and East) is THE archangel to call on for healing and requests to prolong life. The Caduceus, the rod with intertwined snakes used to symbolize medicine, is often associated with Raphael.

The *Malachim*

The order of angels known as the *Malachim* are messengers who bring prophecy and information to those who have reached the level of consciousness represented at *Tiferet*. These angels are beings of communication, moving between universes to transfer information back and forth between deity and creation.

Eternal Soul (*Neshamah*)

Neshamah is the part of the soul which reincarnates from incarnation to incarnation. This is the true "us," existing forever. What is able to be kept from the lower three levels of the soul also stays from one incarnation to the next. This eternal soul remains asleep until we reach some level of spiritual realization, and then awakens. A being that is considered enlightened has their *Neshamah* fully awake and the ruling force of their actions.

Throat Chakra (Located in the middle of the throat)

The throat chakra is the first of the upper chakras, corresponding with the "memory" that binds to the past, but also anchors to facilitate the development and evolution of the soul. This is the center of sound, communication, and speech.

The throat chakra actualizes the intelligence of the heart and gives expression to spirituality. In the book of Genesis, it says that *Elohim* spoke creation into being: "Let there be." The throat chakra is the active power of prophecy, speaking what shall come to pass.

It must be said, however, that when speech is dominated by the three lower chakras and the bestial soul, speech becomes vain and is the cause of suffering. Unconscious speech or negative speech is us trapped in patterns of the past, keeping us in ignorance.

Giving and Receiving

For *Tiferet,* we will focus on a giving and receiving practice (also called *Tonglen* in Buddhist Tradition).

The purpose of Giving and Receiving is to give positive energy to a person or situation. It is also a way of spiritually cleansing energy with your intention.

- Get into a comfortable position.

- Push all thoughts aside and begin to breathe in a regular rhythm.
- Breathe in… and out… in… and out.
- As thoughts arise, gently push them aside and refocus on your breathing.
- Picture your heart filled with light and positive energy–the energy of deity.
- Bring to your mind a person, a situation, or an energy. See it clearly in your mind's eye.
- As you breathe in, picture black smoke coming from the object of your focus.
- Breathe this dark energy in and feel it entering the energy center in your heart.
- As the darkness enters, see it transform to light. Then breathe it back out, into the object of your focus.
- As this process continues, keep breathing the darkness in, and see it continuing to transform to light within your heart.
- As time goes on, less and less dark energy is present, until it is all gone and only light remains.
- Sit in silence and focus on your breath.
- Close with a prayer to whatever deity you feel is appropriate.

Crystal Ball

If you do not have money to purchase items, you can make do with what you have. For instance, a marble or anything spherical can be used for a crystal ball. It does not have to be anything fancy.

The crystal ball can be any spherical object which can be used for scrying (gazing). It is typically made of crystal or stone but symbolically anything spherical can be used. This sphere is compassion (the union of mercy and severity), the symbol of "space", and is an excellent tool for prophecy and vision.

Litha (Summer Solstice)

Although the etymology of the name Litha is not well documented, it may come from Saxon tradition--the opposite of Yule. On this longest day of the year, light and life are abundant. At mid-summer, the sun has reached the moment of his greatest strength. The focus of this festival from a Gnostic Kabbalah perspective is on the enlightenment and liberation of all beings which is the prevue of *Tiferet*.

Sphere 6: Severity

Gevurah (Severity), the sixth sphere, represents restriction. It embodies the act of bringing the divine energy into creation and tempering it so it can be used. Being restriction, *Gevurah* lets darkness and shadow enter creation, but in its extreme restriction becomes cruel, controlling, and hellish. Yet without restriction, the energy of the higher realms would overtake creation and destroy all duality and all beings, returning them to unity with the No Thing (*Ain*) without having gained conscious unity. That would mean no evolution of souls could occur.

Gevurah is one of the most difficult spheres to work with because when restriction goes to its extreme it becomes extremely harsh. It's counterpart, the *Qlipah* of *Golachab* is considered the harshest of the spheres on the Tree of Shadows. *Golachab* means "Flaming Ones" or "Arsonists." Kabbalistic legend teaches the *Qlipoth* emanate from *Gevurah* before it is balanced with *Tiferet* (Beauty), bringing complete restriction and severity. This imbalance creates the entire Tree of Shadows, and thus *Golachab* is the first of the *Qlipoth* to manifest.

Hebrew Name: *Gevurah* (Severity)

Location: Middle of the Left Pillar (Severity)

Hebrew Divine Name: *Elohim Givor* (Severe Gods and Goddesses)

Personality: A Great Warrior

Qlipoth: *Golachab* (The Flaming Ones)

Qlipoth Entity: Ashmedai (Asmodeus)

Aspect of Lilith: Agrat bat Mahlat (the Night Hag)

Deities: Mars, Ares, Bran, Brigid, Minvera, Athena, The Morrigan, Kali, Vulcan, Hephaestes, Ninugurs, Odin, Vali, Indra

Archangel: Kamael

Order of Angels: *Seraphim*

Astrological Attribute: Mars

Level of the Soul: Eternal Soul (*Neshamah*)

Chakra: The Brow

Meditation: Silent Witness

Ritual Topic: Statue and Candle

Holy Day: Lammas

Color: Red

Incense/Plant: Tobacco, Cactus

Elohim Givor

The divine name at this sphere, Elohim Givor, is again a compound name. We have already discussed *Elohim* and its meaning of "God in multiple male and female personalities." *Givor* is a cognate of the Hebrew word, *Gevurah,* which means Severity. Severity in Kabbalah means restriction and is associated with limiting and focusing. This name then can be considered "God of Restriction."

Warriors and Dark Deities

This is the realm of warriors and dark gods and goddesses. Its divinities are the representations of those who fight for their enlightenment and the enlightenment of others. The entities at this level are severe and can appear evil to those not ready to encounter them because of their singular vision supporting transformation at any cost.

Ashmedai **(Asmodeus)**

Ashmedai is the Hebrew name for Asmodeus. He is the king of the *Shedim* – a type of demon who are said to be human souls which were not given human bodies. They were the demons responsible for assisting Solomon with building the Temple. Lilith the Younger is Ashmedai's primary consort, although Na'amah and Agrat bat Mahlat are also associated with him. He is the archdemon of lust, violent fire, and rebellion. A practitioner reaching *Golachab* can break ties to lust and suffering through the power of restriction. This doesn't mean they need to become sexless beings, but they will no longer be egoistically tied to their desires.

Agrat bat Mahlat (the Night Hag)

Agrat bat Mahlat (meaning "Daughter of *Mahlat*"), who is sometimes called *Igaret,* is considered a demoness in Jewish folklore. She is closely related to Lilith and is said to be one of the consorts of Samael. In some tales she is the daughter of Lilith and in others the daughter of Na'amah. She is the youngest of the three, yet usually depicted as a hag. In some lore she is even considered to be Lilith the younger.

According to legend demonic spirits including Agrat were placed inside of a lamp and hidden in a cave near the

Dead Sea. Later the lamp was discovered by King David, and he mated with Agrat, and she bore him a son named Ashmedai (Asmodeus), king of the *Shedim*. Her and the other inhabitants of the lamp were later used by King Solomon to build the Temple. Eventually her power over man was curbed so she could no longer cause havoc and produce demon babies.

Agrat is one of the most wrathful aspects of Lilith, depicted as a hag or a dark void (like a sentient black hole). It is possible to work with Agrat but connecting to her can be difficult and frightening. I have been told of visions of her eating the initiate's body while communicating with them. This points to her nature of devouring husks of darkness and leaving only that which serves. This process can be quite frightening and painful. Agrat is not for the faint of heart, or for any who are just beginning to explore the Dark Mother.

Kamael

The Archangel Kamael is the "burning" angel. He is depicted as a being of fire. Kamael forces the practitioner to look at themselves and decide what within them is good and what is not. If we are ready for Kamael, then he is loving; but if we are not, he will burn us. In legend, Michael is the commander of the holy legions, but Kamael is called God's Champion. The latter does not wage war, but instead consumes everything in his purifying fire until it is completely transformed. Kamael burns husks of darkness away to bring forth what is hidden beneath.

The *Seraphim*

The *Seraphim* are "fiery snakes" and are involved in the process of kundalini within our consciousness. These angels assist us in raising our consciousness and bringing it up through our chakra system. Most *Seraphim* are described as human-shaped with six wings–two covering their faces, two covering their feet, and two to fly with. There are also two other forms of Seraphim, one being a fire dragon and the other being a plague of poisonous fire snakes. These angels exist in the highest planes of existence and shine like the sun.

Brow Chakra (Located at the third eye)

The brow chakra corresponds to our spiritual energetic body and the spiritual worlds. This chakra is the peak of mental consciousness, and it is the center of our sight into higher worlds. Corresponding with light, color, seeing, envisioning, creative imagination, and clairvoyance, the brow is the "seat of the Gnostic Mind."

This chakra is the seat of spiritual knowledge, understanding, and wisdom, yet it still abides in the dualism of mind. This center is the guiding or directing principle of the chakras below it, but also receives and interprets the divine and supernal influxes from above. It is where divine potential is converted into actuality.

Eternal Soul (*Neshamah*)

When the *Neshamah* is awakened the individual begins to orient everything in their life toward authentically being themselves, their true self begins to reign, and they enact their true will. This does not mean the bestial soul does not rise from time to time, but the person is able to recover quickly and refocus on their spiritual path.

Silent Witness

For *Gevurah* we will focus on a meditation of introspection.
The Practice of the Silent Witness is a practice of observing our mental and emotional states. The key to silent witness is non-judgmental self-observation. The practice involves taking some time and thinking about your day or about a particular event. The purpose is to understand yourself better

and consciously choose how to better react in the future. It is important to think about your intention ahead of time. This should be about examining your emotions, thoughts, and reactions.

- Get into a comfortable position.
- Clear your mind and focus on your breath.
- Fill yourself with light and embrace your intention. You are not going to judge–just observe.
- Replay the interaction or day you want to review in your mind.
- You may find it helpful to think of it as a movie or play instead of your reality. This helps you distance from yourself personally and helps alleviate judgment.
- You can also think of it as someone else's experience–maybe someone's whom you care deeply about. How would you react to them instead of yourself? We tend to be harder on ourselves than others.
- Look at the motivations behind your reactions during the event.
- What were the emotions that surrounded these motivations and reactions?
- What events in your past came up?
- How is this connected to past events of your life?
- What would a loved one get out of the interaction if it was them?
- What would you do differently if it happened again?

- Let the emotions and ideas settle.
- Find peace in what has happened and see this as a learning experience.
- Sit in silence and focus on your breath.
- Close with a prayer to whatever deity you feel is appropriate.

Statue and Candle

If you do not have money to purchase items, you can make do with what you have. For instance, a picture, a rock, or a plant representing deity can be used instead of a statue.

The statue or statues on the altar are representations of god or goddess. Pick one which is either your patron or one who fits the intent of the ritual you are about to perform. These figures can be from any culture and can even be statuary not designed to be deities, but something evoking your idea of god or goddess.

During ritual there is typically at least one candle for light and to represent the Mother Spirit and her magic as part of the ceremony. Many times, three candles are used. Symbolically this could be white on the right, black on the left, and red in the center. These three colors and placements stand for the three pillars of the Tree of Life – Severity, Compassion, and Mercy. However, you can use as many or as few candles as you wish if the symbology makes sense to you.

Lammas (Fall)

Lammas is a holiday celebrated in some English-speaking countries in the Northern Hemisphere, usually between August 1st and September 1st. It is a festival to mark the annual wheat harvest and is the first harvest festival of the year. The focus of this festival from a Gnostic Kabbalah point of view is the binding from action of that which does not serve and the harvesting of *Qlipoth*.

Sphere 7: Mercy

Mercy (*Hesed*), the seventh sphere, represents the unbridled energy of *Ain* (No Thing) and pure conscious energy pouring into creation. This may sound like a good thing, and it is, but without restriction there is no differentiation or "self." Mercy and severity need each other for stability. Sphere 5, Beauty (*Tiferet*), is the balance which holds them in equilibrium. *Hesed* is the first sphere to manifest from the supernal triad via the gateway of *Da'at* (Sphere 0 – Knowledge).

The *Qlipah* of *Gha'Agsheblah*, like its bright counterpart, is the first to manifest after the supernal triad of its tree. This sphere represents "the Smiters" which refers to the repeated "attacks" the mage will endure at this level of consciousness. *Gha'Agsheblah* is the last sphere before the soul passes through the gateway of *Da'at* and enters the infernal realm. This *Qlipoth* makes the initiate ready for the next step on their journey by making the differentiation between lust and pain indistinguishable.

Hebrew Name: *Hesed* (Mercy)

Location: Middle of the Right Pillar (Mercy)

Hebrew Divine Name: *El* (God)

Personality: Holy Priest King or Queen

Qlipoth: *Gha'Agsheblah* (The Smiters)

Qlipoth Entity: Ashtaroth

Aspect of Lilith: Belqis (The Queen of Sheba)

Deities: Zeus, Demeter, Osiris, Jupiter, Odin, Nordens

Archangel: Tzadkiel

Order of Angels: *Hashmalim*

Astrological Attribute: Jupiter

Level of the Soul: Eternal Soul (*Neshamah*)

Chakra: The Crown

Meditation: Union with the Mother

Ritual Topic: The Altar

Holy Day: Mabon (Fall Equinox)

Color: Blue

Incense/Plant: Heliotrope, Jasmine Berries, Morning Glory, Opium poppy, Water Lily (blue)

El

El, as we saw previously, is the masculine singular noun beginning the divine name, *Elohim*. *El* means "god" and is typically male, but like anything in Kabbalah, can refer to any personality (*partzufim*) of divinity which has the energy of the sphere. Some scholars believe *El* and *Yahweh* were originally separate deities in ancient Semitic cultures who were syncretized as the same deity as Judaism became monotheistic.

Holy Priest King or Queen

This is the realm of the Holy Priest King or Holy Priestess Queen. He/She is the merciful ruler who takes care of their subjects' physical and spiritual needs. Within us, this is the aspect connecting us to the divine kingdom and helping us to rule our world as a spiritual being.

Ashtaroth

Ashtaroth, originally named *Astarte,* was a Semitic goddess of love and war, much like the Babylonian *Ishtar* and the Sumerian *Inanna*. In the *Goetia* (a form of magic which emphasizes the summoning or calling forth of lesser spirits or demons to make a visible appearance), Ashtaroth, considered the impure Venus, is depicted with the body of a woman and the head of a beast of burden. She has knowledge of the past, present, and future, giving immense knowledge to those who work with her. Ashtaroth is one of the Fallen and thus can convey information on the Fall and the Great Abyss.

Belqis (The Queen of Sheba)

There is much debate whether the Queen of Sheba was a real person or only a mythical character and the location of Sheba has also been debated. It has been identified as the South Arabian Kingdom of Saba (present day Yemen) and with Ethiopia. The biblical account in the Book of Kings states the Queen of Sheba came to Jerusalem with a huge caravan containing gifts for King Solomon. When they met, she presented him with several riddles to solve to prove his worth.

Early Christian scholars equated the Queen of Sheba with the Queen of the South who is mentioned in the Christian New Testament. This correlation led them to believe the biblical Song of Songs was a proclamation of love between the Queen of Sheba and King Solomon, bringing speculation that she became his consort. This is further drawn out in the Ethiopian epic, the *Kebra Nagast,* in which she is a Queen of

Ethiopia who falls in love with Solomon, and they have a child together. Their son brings the Arc of the Covenant from Jerusalem to Ethiopia, so it is preserved before the Temple is destroyed.

Islamic sources name the Queen of Sheba, Belqis, but there are several versions of her story. The name Belqis, which is Arabic, is probably derived from the Hebrew version of a Greek word meaning concubine. Some tales agree with the Christian sources saying she and Solomon were married, while others disagree. Some stories even propose that she was the child of a human and a spirit being, making her not quite human.

Jewish *Midrash* and Kabbalistic sources take the story of the Queen of Sheba much further by equating her with Lilith. In one story Solomon sees her bare legs which are covered in hair, and he immediately knows she is Lilith in disguise. However, most of the *Midrash* still claim Solomon and Belqis have a sexual relationship. In one of these stories, King Nebuchadnezzar of Babylon is their offspring who eventually destroys the Temple and enslaves the Jewish people. In other tales, Solomon uses the *Shedim* to build the Temple. While the construction is happening, Solomon encounters Agrat and enters a sexual union with her as well.

Whether Belqis is associated with Lilith herself or one of her other aspects, in most of the tales there seems to be a genuine relationship between the Queen of Sheba and Solomon, something akin to an actual marriage or at least a loving affair. Solomon is one of the few human men Lilith has a true relationship with instead of in most myths, taking their seed while they sleep show, she can create demon offspring.

Tzadkiel

The Archangel Tzadkiel is the "righteousness of God." This archangel continually grants blessings and mercy to all who seek him. Tzadkiel is also known as the "great angel of the rainbow glory" because of his association with blessings. It may seem Tzadkiel is an easy archangel to approach, but he is not. Because he is the embodiment of *Hesed* (Mercy), he radiates so much energy he is difficult to encounter. If the practitioner has issues with ego grasping or fear, he or she will be overwhelmed by Tzadkiel's presence due to his overwhelming power.

The *Hashmalim*

The *Hashmalim* are called "the Speaking Silences." Even though they do not make sound, they are still able to communicate. Their communication is through dream, vision, and other various methods. At the end of Ezekiel's vision, he states God spoke to him out of silence. In Exodus it says, "all the people saw the words," describing an experience of synesthesia, where senses are manifested through an alternate pathway. Both of these descriptions involve the brain receiving information that comes to them through a sense other than hearing.

Hayyah (Eternal Soul)

The *Hayyah* is the part of the soul which connects the soul within the body (*Nefesh, Ruach,* and *Neshamah*) with the part of the soul outside of creation (*Yechidah*). I often equate this with our "wireless" connection to Ain Sof Or (Endless Light).

Crown Chakra (Located at the top of the head)

The crown center corresponds to the true self as divinity and to the threshold of enlightenment; it is the place of the full generation of an astral body. This center corresponds with our true will, which is supra-conscious. The crown corresponds to transcendence, deep meditation, cessation; enlightenment; and non-dual awareness. In the brow we experience direct knowledge of deity and in the crown, we experience conscious unification with deity.

Union with the Mother

For *Hesed,* we will focus on a meditation which shows our Union with the Mother Goddess.

The basic aim in all meditations with the Mother (in any of her forms) is to embody her in yourself and to commune with her, receiving messages she has to give.

- Sit in a place where you will not be disturbed and let yourself settle in.
- From this place of consciousness, shift your focus to the light in your heart, envisioning it illuminating your whole body. Let your mind and heart turn to the Mother and pray she might come and be with you. Then, envision a ray of light streaming forth from your heart– leaping out of you like a shooting star–and the Image of the Mother appearing in the space before you.
- Select any embodiment of the Mother you wish to work with (Lilith, Hecate, etc.). Chant the name of the Goddess. Picture her reaching out to you and giving you messages and teachings only for you. When she is finished speaking, envision her turning to light and

pouring back into your heart as light. Thank her for her presence and what she has told you.

- At first, don't focus on any surroundings or any detail beyond the Mother's presence with you. Once you have practiced this meditation, you can begin to add details to the environment and location, as well as details of the experience.
- Close in praise of the Mother.

Altar

If you do not have money to purchase items, you can make do with what you have. For instance, your altar can be something you set up and take down as needed, or you can use a box with a cloth thrown over it.

Altar arrangement is up to the individual, but it is a place you will want to keep your ritual tools and some type of image of deity. Other items can be put on the altar, such as crystals, fetishes, etc.

I usually put the statue in the back–in the middle with one image or one to the left and one to the right with two images. I place the cup and knife to the left and the wand and pentacle to the right. The crystal ball can either go in the center or sit on the pentacle. But you can arrange your altar as you feel drawn.

To consecrate your altar, anoint every item with oil and pray they are bound to you and the workings you are trying to do. Light the candles on the altar and smudge it with either sage or incense, seeing the power of magick entering and surrounding everything to build it into a cohesive whole.

If your living situation is such that you cannot have an open altar, I suggest getting a box that will act as the base of the altar, that you can put all your items when they are not being used for easy storage.

Mabon (Fall Equinox)

Mabon is a feast of thanksgiving, a celebration of the Earth's bounty. And as with all Holy Days, the cycles of the seasons mirror the cycles of our lives. Mabon is a time to reflect and wrap things up. The focus of this feast from a Gnostic Kabbalah standpoint is mercy, expressed by the light from above flowing down into creation.

Sphere 8: Understanding

Sphere 8 is understanding (*Binah*) and represents the archetypical forms of creation. Understanding is outside of space and time but is also the womb of creation where all the other spheres dwell, just as a fetus resides in the mother. The sphere of *Binah* is called a Palace in Kabbalah because the King dwells here, but once the sphere is arrayed with the force of creation, Binah becomes a house where the divine family lives.

Satariel, the *Qlipothic* side of *Binah,* is also called "The Concealers." *Binah* and *Satariel* are the first spheres in their respective trees past the abyss of *Da'at*. *Satariel* is a dark sphere of hidden knowledge and mysteries. *Binah* is the home of Mother God and *Satariel* is said to be the primordial abode of Lilith, but she descends to the lower realms and works the astral planes to transform reality.

Hebrew Name: *Binah* (Understanding)

Location: Top of the Left Pillar (Severity)

Hebrew Divine Name: *Elohim* (God and Goddesses)

Personality: Mother, Form of Creation

Qlipoth: *Satariel* (The Concealers)

Qlipoth Entity: Lucifuge

Aspect of Lilith: Lilith the Elder

Deities: Isis, Hecate, Danu, Demeter, Tiamat, Kishar, Asherah, Atira, Nut

Archangel: Tzafkiel

Order of Angels: *Aralim*

Astrological Attribute: Saturn

Level of the Soul: *Yechidah*

Chakra: Supernal

Meditation: Middle Pillar

Ritual Topic: Kabbalistic Ritual

Holy Day: Samhain

Color: Black

Incense/Plant: Myrrh, Cypress

Elohim

We have previously seen the divine name *Elohim* as a portion of other divine names at lower spheres. You will recall *Elohim* is typically associated with "God with multiple male and female personalities." In Kabbalah, *Elohim* is Mother God who is pregnant with the whole of creation.

Mother God

The personality at this sphere is Mother God. She is the Mother goddess in all her aspects as the form of creation. *Aima,* Mother, is the personality of deity at *Binah*. The Mother goddesses are the most active in creation because they are the wombs which birth enlightenment and tend to creation. *Abba,* Father, is typically more distant and untouchable, especially in Kabbalistic tradition.

Lucifuge

Lucifuge should not be confused with *Lucifer,* the Light Bringer. Lucifuge hides from the Light and transverses the dark labyrinth of *Satariel*. This symbolizes his ability to look into a soul's darkness and show the mage very clearly what needs to be transformed. He is also known as the Lord of Pacts. Because Lucifuge is a being of darkness, the best way to work with him is to put out all lights in your meditation space, light one black candle, and call out to Lucifuge to come and allow you to see there what needs to be altered.

Lilith the Elder

As we discussed at *Yesod,* some Kabbalistic *Midrash* discusses two Liliths, Lilith the Younger and Lilith the Elder. Most writings, however. only talk of one Lilith and do not mention younger or elder. Since Lilith is usually associated with Samael and not discussed as having angelic parents, it is assumed most texts are discussing Lilith the Elder. This Lilith is the first wife of Adam, the partner of Samael, the sometimes consort of God, and eventually an enlightened goddess. Lilith at the level of *Binah* is the Dark Mother who brings transformation to all of creation.

Tzafkiel

As the Archangel of compassionate understanding, Tzafkiel leads the angels who send the spiritual energy of understanding to people. Tzafkiel helps people learn more about deity, sends them insights about themselves, and guides them to make decisions in their daily lives that reflect their core identities.

Tzafkiel is said to hold the Book of Life, which is the list of all enlightened beings in this cosmic cycle (throughout time). This archangel appears during meditation as the night sky clothed in dark clouds.

The *Aralim*

The *Aralim* are the order of angels who dwell in *Binah*. The *Aralim* are called Thrones, and they are the strength and stability of *Binah*. It is interesting to note that an older, alternative name for Binah was *Khorsia,* which means "throne." This order of angels gives authority and power to spirits and humans.

Divine Spark *(Yechidah)*

The *Yechidah* is the part of every being which is beyond creation and completely part of the divine realm. When this part of the soul is completely awake, a being reaches full enlightenment and liberation because they are connected back to the universe of *Adam Kadmon,* outside of time and space.

Supernal Chakra

The Supernal Chakra (Located above the head) is not part of our internal energy centers and is not located in our body. The Supernal Chakra is in unity with *Ain*, *Ain Sof*, and *Ain Sof Or* beyond creation. This Chakra is only activated with complete enlightenment and resides outside of time/space.

Middle Pillar

For the sphere of *Binah* we will focus on a meditation called Middle Pillar which will activate your chakras.

- Get into a comfortable position.
- Push all thoughts aside and begin to breathe in a regular rhythm.
- Breathe in… and out… in… and out.
- As thoughts arise, gently push them aside and refocus on your breathing.
- Picture your heart filled with light and positive energy–the energy of deity.
- Envision a sphere of brilliant white light, translucent and clear, above your head. Visualize and feel this center of supernal light there, above your head. Awaken this center of divine energy with the intonation of the divine name:
    - Omoroca.
- Then envision the light descending through your head down to your throat, forming another sphere of light at your throat, a sphere of translucent lavender light, brightly shining. Awaken this center of divine energy with the intonation of the divine name:
    - Lilith.
- Let the light continue its descent down through your body to form another sphere of light in the middle of

your torso at your solar plexus, a sphere of translucent golden light which shines brightly like the sun. Awaken this divine center with the intonation of the divine name:

  - Norea

- Envision the light naturally and spontaneously continuing its descent, forming another sphere of translucent violet light at your groin, a vibrant and brightly shining center of divine energy. Awaken this divine center with the intonation of the divine name:
  - Lilit
- Let the light complete its descent, passing down to your feet and forming a sphere of radiant darkness there, as though a radiant indigo or obsidian black translucent light, all receiving. Awaken this divine center of energy with the intonation of the divine name:
  - Na'amah
- Having brought the supernal light down, envision and feel an awakening and upward rush of divine energy from the depths of your consciousness, as though from the secret center of the Earth there is a response from below to the power coming from above. Envision yourself becoming like an inexhaustible fountain of this energy, the light rushing up in ascent from the base of your feet, through your spine and out the top of your

head, as though through a pipe of light formed in your subtle body.

- Circulate this light throughout your aura with your breath. As you exhale, visualize, and feel the light pouring down the front of your body. As you inhale, visualize, and feel it ascending up the back side of your body. Continue this focus until the current flowing down the front of your body and up the back is well established, as though the flow continues on its own.
- Then shift to a focus upon another current of light simultaneously flowing down your left side and up the right side of your body, using your breath as before to circulate the energy, your exhalation bringing it down the left side and inhalation bringing it up the right side. Continue in this focus until the current is fully established.
- Now envision your body as a body of light, as though every particle is self-luminous. And visualize and feel a sphere of brilliant light surrounding you, a radiant aura of golden-white translucent light.
- When this is complete you can proceed to further prayer, meditation, or ritual, or close the session by completely absorbing and grounding the energy-intelligence generated by the practice. This, then, completes the Middle Pillar Meditation.

Kabbalistic Ritual

For the Sphere of *Binah* we will perform a ritual.

Invoking Lilith

This ritual is performed to invoke Lilith into your physical space rather than just in a meditative state.

The Ritual

For this ritual you will need four candles: one white, one black, one red, and one purple. You will also need incense (sandalwood, rose, or Night Queen is best) and an athame (a ritual knife). Have an altar in the center of the room with an image of Lilith on it.

In the East place the white candle (you can also add a clear quartz crystal or anything which reminds you of Lilith the Younger–a statue, picture, etc.).

In the West place the black candle (you can also add a smokey quartz crystal or anything which reminds you of the Sumerian Lilitu–a statue, picture, etc.).

In the South place the red candle (you can also add a rose quartz crystal or anything which reminds you of Lilith the Elder–a statue, picture, etc.).

In the North place the purple candle (you can also add an amethyst crystal or anything which reminds you of Na'amah– a statue, picture, etc.).

Light the incense and the candles (East, then West, then South, then North).

Face the East and use the athame to outline an invoking pentagram and intone, "Lilith, Lilith, Lilith."

Turn and face the West and use the athame to outline an invoking pentagram and intone, "Lilit, Lilit, Lilit" (alternately, you can use Agrat bat Mahlat).

Turn and face the South and use the athame to outline an invoking pentagram and intone, "Lilitu, Lilitu, Lilitu" (alternatively, you can use Ardat Lili).

Turn and face the North and use the athame to outline an invoking pentagram and intone, "Na'amah, Na'amah, Na'amah."

Face the center and put the Athame on your altar. Say the following:
"Lilith, daughter of the moon, I call you."
"Lilith, mother of darkness, I call you."
"Lilith, queen of night, I call you."

"I call you, Lilith, to be here with me."
"I come to you as your servant, as your child, asking you to come and be here with me."

Close your eyes and focus on your breathing as if you were in meditation.

Give praise to Lilith and thank her for her presence.
Listen to any messages she has.
Give her your wishes and desires.
"I thank you for your presence."
"I thank you for being my mother and queen."

Pick up the athame.
Face the North and use the athame to outline a banishing pentagram and intone, "Na'amah, Na'amah, Na'amah."

Face the South and use the athame to outline a banishing pentagram and intone, "Lilitu, Lilitu, Lilitu" (alternatively, you can use Ardat Lili).

Face the West and use the athame to outline a banishing pentagram and intone, "Lilit, Lilit, Lilit" (alternately, you can use Agrat bat Mahlat).

Face the East and use the athame to outline a banishing pentagram and intone, "Lilith, Lilith, Lilith."

Say, "As it is spoken, so it is done."

You can extinguish the flame.

Embodying Lilith

As an additional step in this ritual after listening to Lilith's message for you, you may want to say the following:

"Mother Lilith, I truly desire to be one of your Lilin (if you identify as female, Lilu if you identify as male). I wish to embody you in heart, mind, and soul. Make me yours and of your purpose so I may find enlightenment and liberation from the cycle of rebirth. Not so I may rest, but so I may come back in every generation to help the outcast and the marginalized to find their way, as you have done since the beginning of time."

"Make me yours and mark me for your ascension."

This vow is not to be taken lightly. This is the vow to reincarnate until this cosmic cycle is over as a being who helps those who are alone to find their way in the world and in their spiritual life. This is the same as the Buddhist bodhisattva vow. Once this is sealed, there is no going back.

This concludes the ritual.

Samhain (Festival of the Dead)

As October turns to November the sacred time of Samhain (Festival of the Dead) arrives. Samhain means "Summer's End" and pronounced saa-win (Gaelic) or saa-ween (Welsh), Samhain is a celebration of the end of the harvest and the start of the coldest half of the year. For many practitioners, myself included, Samhain also heralds the beginning of the spiritual new year. For Gnostic Kabbalists, this Feast of the Dead is focused on helping all spirits to move on either to their next incarnation or to move on to their afterlife.

Sphere 9: Wisdom

Sphere 9 is Wisdom (*Hokmah*), the force of creation, considered male and is akin to the force of deity's will to create. In Greek, the word for wisdom is *Sophia* and it is considered female, which makes it more akin to the sphere of *Binah*. *Hokmah,* considered to be very distant from creation, cannot be known completely while incarnate, however limited experience of *Hokmah* can be brought back and partially conceptualized during meditation and ritual. It is a sphere of pure thought, and the force of creative will.

The *Qlipah* at Sphere 9 is *Ghagiel,* the Hinderers. The dark phallic Gods such as the Devil at his most masculine rule *Ghagiel*. This is the active sphere of will of the Tree of Shadows where the magickal practitioner's will is tested. *Ghagiel* is called the Hinderers because every test which can stop his or her determination is put before the practitioner to hone their will to be the force needed to obtain full realization at the pinnacle of the tree.

Hebrew Name: *Hokmah* (Wisdom)

Location: Top of the Right Pillar (Mercy)

Hebrew Divine Name: *Yahweh* (He who was, is, and shall be– Father, Mother, Son, and Daughter)

Personality: Father, Force of Creation

Qlipoth: *Ghagiel* (The Hinderers)

Qlipoth Entity: Beelzebub

Aspect of Lilith: Obizuth

Deities: Zeus, Jupiter, Great Pan, Osiris, The Dagda, Cernnunnos, Enki, Ashur, Ivarog, Geb

Archangel: Ratziel

Order of Angels: *Ofanim*

Astrological Attribute: The Zodiac

Level of the Soul: *Yechidah*

Chakra: Supernal

Meditation: Be the Night

Ritual: Communion with Lilith

Holy Day: Full Moon Esbat

Color: Grey

Incense/Plant: Musk, Amaranth

Yahweh

We have previously seen the divine name *Yahweh* as a portion of other divine names at lower spheres. You will recall *Yahweh* means "He who was, is, and shall be." *Yahweh* is also associated with the idea of Father God. The primary Kabbalistic *partzufim*, personalities of God, are all represented in the letters of the name *Yahweh–Yod* (Father), *Heh* (Mother), *Vav* (Son), and *Heh* (Daughter/Bride).

Father God

The personality at this Sphere is Father God (*Abba*). He is the Father in all his forms as the force of creation. He is outside the other spheres and only "touches" the sphere of *Binah* through the force of his creative will. Because Father God is so far from human realization, he is often pictured as a bearded king only seen in profile.

Beelzebub

Beelzebub, also known as Lord of the Flies, was originally a Phoenician God known as *Beelsebel*, meaning "Lord of Lords." He is considered one of the Princes of Hell in *Goetic* teachings. As Lord of the Flies, Beelzebub feasts on the old world, to create the new. Our perceptions and worldview are shattered and reborn under our own will. Just as *Yahweh* is Father beyond all, Beelzebub is the dark Father beyond the *Qlipoth* in creation.

Obizuth

In the Testament of Solomon, a demon named Obizuth appears to King Solomon, saying "I am a fierce spirit of myriad names and shapes." She says she travels the world at night to torment women in childbirth, giving them increased pain and putting their life at risk. She is described as having a greenish complexion, long snake-like hair, and a body hidden in darkness. Interestingly, her demeanor is bright and cheerful. From my experience of her, Obizuth is Lilith under one of her myriad names and faces that she assumes, depending on her place on either Tree.

Obizuth is not mentioned outside of Solomonic texts. The Testament of Solomon is estimated to have been written around the 2nd Century BCE making this one of the earliest texts equating Lilith with difficult childbirth. Obizuth is associated with this sphere because of her elusive nature. It would seem that a being who torments mothers would not be at the top of the Tree, but this description of her is actually a foil to the fact she represents change through turmoil and the birthing of new incarnations.

Ratziel

The Archangel Ratziel is said to have a book called the "Book of Ratziel," containing the knowledge of everything. This is, of course, not a physical book, but the consciousness of Ratziel (there is a published book called the *Book of Ratziel,* but this is not the same text). Since Ratziel is outside of time and space, he can see all that has, is, and will happen (which is much like the Akashic Records).

The *Ofanim*

The order of angels called *Ofanim,* are "Wheels" which are very, very different than angels portrayed in Western pop-culture. In the Jewish Scriptures, the Book of Ezekiel describes "wheels within wheels." These are the *Ofanim.* These wheels represent the turning of time, space, and the zodiac. Before modern Kabbalah, there was an early form of Kabbalistic mysticism called *Merkavah,* Throne Chariot Mysticism. The *Ofanim* are some of the primary angels of this mystic path.

Be the Night

Lilith is associated with a number of different archetypes, but the night is one of the most prevalent themes in all her mythology and iconography. This is partly due to her time in the Land of *Nod,* where there is eternal twilight. When she leaves Adam and the Garden and flies off to *Nod,* she transforms into a creature of darkness. The following practice is designed to help connect us with Lilith's nocturnal nature.

Go outside in the nighttime and find a comfortable spot to sit. Somewhere in nature is ideal, but anywhere you can see the sky will work, even in your yard or on a balcony. It is best to perform this practice on a clear or at least semi-clear evening when you can see the moon and/or stars.

- Look up into the night sky and notice whatever you can about it. Take in the immenseness of its dark canopy and all the details that come to your attention.
- Once you feel like you have taken in as much as you can, sit back and relax.
- Breathe in and out, feeling your toes, feet, and ankles relax.
- Continue to breathe and feel your calves, knees, and thighs relax.
- Breathe in and out, pushing all thoughts aside.
- Feel your fingers, hands, and wrists relax.

- Breathe in and out, continuing to focus only on your breath.
- Feel your lower arms, elbows, and upper arms relax.
- As you breathe, feel your body becoming light and floating.
- Feel your pelvis, abdomen, and chest relax.
- Breathe in and out, continuing to push any thoughts out of the way.
- Feel your shoulders, neck, and head relax.
- Abide in your breath.
- After a time feel your body begin to expand and at the same time become more and more buoyant.
- You feel your body becoming one with the sky.
- Your body is as black as the void of space and empty of anything except oneness. You are the darkness of space.
- As you abide, you start to feel your heart opening–at first just a crack--and light begins to pour from the crescent of the lower portion of your heart.
- As you continue to breathe, your heart expands until your heart is the waxing moon, opening and opening with each breath.
- You continue to be the void of space, but your heart opens completely as the full moon, shining down upon the earth with silver light.
- Feel the darkness of your body being energized by the moon which is at your heart.

- Lights begin to shine all over your black form, as stars burst into light across the horizon.
- Abide in your breath and feel yourself as the non-dual nature of the sky, darkness and light joined in perfect harmony.
- When you feel you have spent enough time realizing this non-duality, begin to bring your consciousness back to this world.
- Breathe in and out and feel yourself recede from the sky and return to a physical, human manifestation.
- Wiggle your toes, move your body, and return to your normal consciousness.

As you go about your life in the coming days, remember being the sky full of darkness and light.

Communion of Lilith

The practice of using food and drink for ritual is an incredibly old one. It is best known in Christian Tradition where the partaking of bread and wine is used in the sacrament of Communion or Eucharist. There are varying ideas on what this ritual means in Christianity; Catholics believe the elements become the actual body and blood of Jesus through what is called Transubstantiation, while Protestants typically believe the act is symbolic and a remembrance. There are

Traditions which consider the communion to be anything in between these two ideas.

The thing most people do not know is that the practice of partaking of bread and wine is much older than what is portrayed in the New Testament. In the book of Genesis in the *Torah,* Abraham and Sarah participate in a remarkably similar ritual overseen by the enigmatic priest-king *Melchizedek.* But this example was not the only time such a ritual was performed. The Pharaoh Akhenaten held daily bread and wine ceremonies in ancient Egypt to worship the Aten (the deity represented by the sun disk).

The communion below is based in Gnostic and Kabbalistic Tradition and bridges the Catholic Transubstantiation and the Protestant remembrance. In no way do I suggest the host becomes Lilith's body, but instead the bread becomes an energetic movement of her darkness, and the wine becomes an energetic movement of her light. We bring both elements together and ingest them to help us embody her by bringing her energy into us. This ritual can be invoked by a solitary practitioner or in a group (gluten free bread can be used for anyone who is gluten sensitive, and grape juice can be used for anyone who cannot partake of alcohol).

Kabbalistic Cross:
Atoh (above head)
Io Adonai (at throat)
Malkut (at feet)
Ve-Gevurah (right shoulder)
Ve-Gedulah (left shoulder)
La-Olam (hands at center)
Amen (hands folded)

Calling of the Mothers:
(face the directions specified)

(East)
Intone: Lilith, Lilith, Lilith
Lilith, Mother of Compassion, we call upon you to bring your power of transformation.

(West)
Intone: Lilit, Lilit, Lilit
Lilit, Mother of Night, we call upon you to bring your power of ancient knowledge.

(South)
Intone: Lilitu, Lilitu, Lilitu
Lilitu, Mother of Antiquity, we call upon you to bring your power of Illumination.

(North)
Intone: Na'amah, Na'amah, Na'amah
Na'amah, Mother of Seduction, we call upon you to bring your power of creation.

Invocation of the Archangels:
(East)
Intone: Raphael, Raphael, Raphael
Raphael, Healing Power of God, we invite you and we welcome you; please come and be with us!

(West)
Intone: Gabriel, Gabriel, Gabriel
Gabriel, Strength of God, we invite you and welcome you; please come and be with us!

(South)
Intone: Michael, Michael, Michael
Michael, Who is like unto God, we invite you and welcome you; please come and be with us!

(North)
Intone: Uriel, Uriel, Uriel
Uriel, Light of God, we invite you and we welcome you; please come and be with us!

(Center--Up)

Intone: Metatron, Metatron, Metatron
Metatron, Archangel of Father energy, we invite you and we welcome you; please come and be with us!

(Center--Down)
Intone: Sandalfon, Sandalfon, Sandalfon
Sandalfon, Archangel of Mother energy, we invite you and we welcome you; please come and be with us!

(Hands on altar)
Intone: Hua, Hua, Hua
Hua, Archangel of Enlightenment, we invite you and we welcome you; please come and be with us!

O Mother of Darkness,
O Mother of Light,
Lilith,
We open our mind, heart, and life to you,
We invite you and we welcome you,
Come, rest upon us.
Come, and indwell us!

Transform us now with your power,
And in Union with you, let us be your hands and feet,
To abide in your dark embrace

"This is *your* body *of darkness,*" "this is *your* blood *of light*" and "*we* do this in remembrance of *you.*"
Blessed is Lilith's body which is darkness.
Blessed is Lilith's blood which is light.

I am a child of Lilith; a being of darkness and light; I bring balance and compassion by knowing separation and unity. We stand for the outcast and marginalized; we stand up for justice; in remembrance of Lilith, let us partake.

Break the bread into small pieces and then perform the sign of the circled even armed cross (a symbol of unity) over both the bread and wine, and then say:

Mother Lilith, bless these elements with your darkness and your light so we may partake and be one with you.
(The person officiating the ritual takes a piece of bread and dips into the wine. He or she then ingests it and invokes Lilith's energy to enter them. If others are present the officiant picks up the bread platter and wine glass and offers the elements to the next person. After they partake, they then take the platter and glass and offer to the next person until it goes around the circle.)

Let us send this darkness and light into all realms, worlds, and universes in the name of Our Mother.

May the balance of light and dark be given to all: May all beings be healed; May all living spirits and souls find their unification. May all become their true selves.

As it is spoken, so is it done.

Full Moon Esbat

Up until now, the holy days discussed have all been Sabbats, which are focused on the solar calendar. Those 8 holidays are based on the Earth's rotation around the sun and the seven *Sephirot* in creation, plus Sphere 8, *Binah,* which is the womb holding creation. This holy day, however, is based on Full Moons when Lilith is the Mother who brings transformation through our magick and practice. Any ritual performed under the full moon is filled with mercy and compassion.

Sphere 10: Crown

Keter means crown which represents the divine energy beyond creation and just at the tip of the No Thing (*Ain*). This Sphere is all potential and both male and female, but any form of deity at this level is unknowable in earthly understanding because this is far beyond normal consciousness. Any deities associated with *Keter* must come down the Tree to really be experienced in a way our human body and mind can comprehend. We may experience them in our super-conscious state, but there will be no words or symbols which can really be translated directly.

The *Qlipah* at this level is called *Thaumiel,* "The Twin Gods." It is symbolized by Satan and Moloch facing opposite directions. These entities are polar opposites and represent duality. Satan, the adversary, faces backward to look at what has been rejected by the practitioner while Moloch, the king, faces forward to look at what the practitioner is now able to create. At this level, the mage has become a fully enlightened being who is still individuated and whole.

Hebrew Name: *Keter* (Crown)

Location: Top of the Central Pillar (Compassion)

Hebrew Divine Name: *Ehieh*

Personality: Ancient of Days (Ancient King or Queen in Profile)

Qlipoth: *Thaumiel* (The Twin Gods)

Qlipoth Entity: Lucifer

Aspect of Lilith: Omoroca

Deities: Supernal Hecate, Ptah, Gaea, Jumala, Nipara, Nohochacyum

Archangel: Metatron

Order of Angels: *Hayyot Ha-Kodesh*

Astrological Attribute: Beginning of all Cycles

Level of the Soul: *Yechidah*

Chakra: Supernal

Meditation: Unification Meditation

Ritual Topic: Summoning the Lilin

Holy Day: Black Moon Esbat

Color: White

Incense/Plant: Ambergris, Almond Flower

Ehieh

Ehieh means "I Am," and is the first thought which creates anything outside of the No Thing (*Ain*). At the burning bush, Moses asks for God's name and is told *Ehieh Asher Ehieh,* which means "I Am Who I Am" or "I Am Who I Shall Be." This idea sums up in one sentence the whole manifestation of the Tree of Life, the Tree of Shadows, and the purpose of creation in it describes The Nothing (*Ain*) becoming something (*Ani*) and returning in a conscious state of Endless Light (*Ain Sof Or*).

Ancient of Days

The Divine Image of an ancient King or Queen helps to illustrate that *Keter* was the first *Sephirah* to be manifested after creation of this cosmic cycle. Thus, anything of *Keter* is truly ancient and on the verge of truly eternal.

Lucifer

Lucifer's throne is located at *Thamiel,* and he is the entity of this *Qlipah*. Lucifer in myth was originally a Greco-Roman solar deity known as the Light-bearer. This epitaph comes from his association with the planet Venus, the morning star that rises before the sun. The Latin version of the Bible, the Vulgate, translated morning star as Lucifer. Because of this translation, the primary fallen angel who is considered to be the Devil, also became known as Lucifer.

Satan, or "adversary," is a title in Jewish religion and not the name of a particular being. Any entity who acts as an accuser of humanity is called a Satan. The primary being in Judaism who held this title is Samael. Because of Lucifer's association as a fallen angel, he and Samael became the same being in western consciousness.

Lucifer has become the Devil, the Satan, and the chief fallen angel from the viewpoint of Western culture. Thus, he is god of *Thaumiel* and the symbol of the dark enlightenment one reaches at this Sphere.

Omoroca

Omoroca is the aspect of Lilith beyond creation and beyond time, space, and human understanding. She is the great dragon of the void which is the first desire of creation and the chaos which sparks all. Omoroca is pure darkness, consciousness with no restraint. Omoroca's name is found in Mesopotamian lore describing her as having a similar presentation to the dragon goddess *Tiamat*.

Metatron

In the book of Genesis, the story of Enoch is given:

> "When Enoch had lived sixty-five years, he became the father of Methuselah. Enoch walked with God after the birth of Methuselah three hundred years and had sons and daughters. Thus, all the days of Enoch were three hundred sixty-five years. Enoch walked with God, then he was no more, because God took him."

This is all which is written about Enoch in Genesis. The paragraph asserts that Enoch never dies but is somehow taken up to higher universes. In *Midrash,* Enoch becomes the archangel Metatron. Metatron is the highest angel, representing the souls of all enlightened beings in this cosmic cycle. Metatron can be considered the fully realized version of Sandalfon who is beyond time and space.

Hayyot Ha-Kodesh (Holy Living Creatures)

The *Hayyot Ha-Kodesh,* called "Holy Living Creatures," are said to stand directly in the inner presence of deity. They are entities so otherworldly that they have a very alien presence. This order of angels transmits the intelligence of enlightenment to all who have evolved into their true self and the ability to experience beyond the five senses.

Unification Meditation

The aim of this meditation is to join with the consciousness of everything in and beyond creation.

- Sit in a place where you will not be disturbed and perform primordial meditation.
- Picture yourself floating in the night sky. The sky is black and full of stars. You are comfortable and at peace as you float silently.
- You see a black bird, like a raven, flying overhead and coming toward you.
- The bird turns into black light when it reaches the space just above your head. See and feel it pour down through your physical form into your energy body.
- As the black light reaches your heart, feel it spread out and fill your whole spiritual body. It fills you completely with its cool, dark power.
- As you are taken up in the darkness, feel your mind settle into the void, empty of all anxiety and concerns. Feel your connection to everything and to nothing at the same time.

- After some time, feel the darkness coalesce into your heart, collapsing into a singularity, a grain of energy hidden yet ever present.
- Return to normal consciousness and feel yourself return to your body.

The meditation is complete, but an essence of the void will always be in you.

Summoning the Lilin

This ritual is performed to call Lilith's children, the Lilin, to come to protect and guide the summoner. The Lilin can be somewhat chaotic just like Lilith, so make sure you have worked with Lilith for some time before using this ritual.

<u>The Ritual</u>
For this ritual you will need a black or red candle and incense (sandalwood, rose, or Night Queen is best).

Light the incense and candle.

Perform the Kabbalistic Cross in front of the Altar.

- Atoh (above head)
- Io Adonai (at throat)
- Malkut (at feet)
- Ve-Gevurah (right shoulder)

- Ve-Gedulah (left shoulder)
- La-Olam (hands at center)
- Amen (hands folded)

- Intone – "Lilith, Lilith, Lilith"
- Say the following –
    - Queen of Night; Mother of Darkness; Goddess of those Abandoned.
    - I come before you as your child, waiting upon your presence.
    - I seek for you to bring your children, The Lilin, to guide and protect me.
    - I am your child and I seek your daughters to come and be with me.

- Chant – "Lilith, Lilith, Lilith" as many times as needed.
- When you feel connected to her spirit, envision Lilith standing in front of you.
- She is bathed in darkness. All you see is her face, with her hair and wings obscuring everything else.
- In the darkness you start to see eyes appear. These are her children, the *Lilin*.
- The *Lilin* rule over many things: protection, death, graveyards, the sea, and much more.
- Within your soul, call to the one *Lilin* who is meant to protect and guide you. Do not make assumptions about which *Lilin* will answer.

- One by one, the eyes blink out, but one pair brightens and a *Lilin* steps forward. This is your guide and protector.

- Say the following:
    - Thank you, my Mother, for bringing my sister to me.
    - Thank you, my Queen, for giving me a guide and protector.
    - As it is spoken, so it is done.

The ritual is complete. You can blow out the candle and know you now have a spiritual guide and protector who will be with you for the rest of this incarnation.

Black Moon Esbat

As with Hokmah, the holy day for Keter is based on the Moon, however this time we are working with the black moon. At this phase, Lilith manifests as crone and vampire, one who brings transformation through difficult times and shadow work. Any ritual performed under the black moon is filled with compassion and severity.

Sphere 0: Knowledge

Da'at, or Knowledge, is not a *Sephirah. The Sefer Yetzirah,* a source work of Kabbalah, states the *Sephirot* number 10, not 9 and not 11. *Da'at* is often called the hidden *Sephirah* or the non-*Sephirah* – it is the concealed aspect of Tiferet (and its corresponding *Qlipah*), and the revealed aspect of *Keter* (and its corresponding *Qlipah*). *Da'at* is a gateway which crosses universes, and which exists between the Tree of Life and the Tree of Shadows. *Da'at* in Hebrew has the same meaning as *Gnosis* in Greek: experiential knowledge.

Hebrew Name: *Da'at* (Knowledge)

Location: Between Crown (*Keter*) and Beauty (*Tiferet*) on the Central Pillar

Hebrew Divine Name: *Yahweh Elohim*

Personality: Angel of the Pit

Qlipoth: *Da'at* (The Abyss)

Qlipoth Entity: Abbadon

Aspect of Lilith: Eishet Zununim

Deities: Hecate, Lilith, Na'amah, Arddur, Osiris, Sacred Death, Nephthys, Anubis, Kali

Archangel: Abbadon

Astrological Attribute: Neptune

Level of the Soul: Peak of the upper *Ruach*; Base of the *Neshamah*

Chakra: Between Crown and Supernal

Meditation: Meditation of the Void

Ritual Topic: Soul Eclipse

Color: Clear

Incense/Plant: Sage, Wormwood

Yahweh Elohim

The divine name of *Da'at* in Kabbalah combines the divine names of Sphere 9 (*Hokmah*) and Sphere 8 (*Binah*). *Yahweh Elohim* represents the combination of Father and Mother God so that creation can manifest from their union.

***Abbadon* (Angel and Demon of the Pit)**

The archangel and archdemon of *Da'at* is Abaddon, called the angel and the demon of the pit. This revelation shows reality is not dualistic but subject to our consciousness. How

Abaddon appears to us is based on our expectations and the state of our ego. If we are ready to pass through the gate of *Da'at* to move closer to our enlightenment and liberation, then Abaddon is a beautiful being who assists us. If we are not ready and still self-grasping, then Abaddon will be a horrible monster who will seem to be trying to destroy us.

Eishet Zununim

Eishet Zununim, called "the Woman of Whoredom", is described as one of the spirits of prostitution along with Lilith, Na'amah, and Agrat bat Mahlat. Eishet, associated with Egypt, is also one of the wives of Samael. Her title is sometimes *Kodeshah,* which is based on the Hebrew word *Kodesh,* meaning sacred, indicating she is a sacred prostitute. Her associations point to her being an aspect of Lilith – one of her many faces. *Da'at,* the gate between realms, accepts all who are ready, much as the stereotype of a "whore" is that they will accept any who come to them.

Peak of the upper Ruach; Base of the Neshamah. Between Crown and Supernal Chakra

Within **us *Da'at* is the link between the spirit and the eternal soul. It is** the linkage between who we are and who we can be, and thus its chakra is between our crown and the supernal beyond our incarnation.

Meditation of the Void

The aim of this meditation is to prepare to cross into the void.

- Sit in a place where you will not be disturbed and perform primordial meditation.
- Picture yourself on the shore of a black stream with the night sky above.
- Look inside yourself and see if there are any aspects of yourself which are hidden. Speak these out to Mother Lilith, who is with you in spirit.
- Once everything has been spoken, slowly walk out into the stream. It should only come up to below your knees.
- Feel the gentle flow of water and know the stream connects to a river and then the sea, which is the abyss of Da'at.
- Feel the connection, and then step back onto the shore.
- Return to normal consciousness and feel yourself return to your body.
- The meditation is complete, but an essence of the void will always be in you.

Soul Eclipse

WARNING: I would not recommend this ritual until you have done the work of all the other *Sephirot*. You also must be very sure you wish to dedicate yourself to Lilith for life (or longer).

The ritual of Soul Eclipse is performed to remove the shadow (the part of you which is not really you) from your soul and replace it with the image of Lilith. After this ritual is complete, you are bound to her as her child and devotee. Again, do not do this practice if you have any doubts about your connection with the Dark Mother.

The Ritual

For this practice you will need two candles. One should be bright (preferably white), and the other should be dark (preferably black). You will also need a cloak or covering (this can be a prayer shawl/Tallit, a scarf, or even a light blanket) and a black mirror (a crystal or regular mirror can be substituted).

Have incense burning before you begin (sandalwood, rose, or Night Queen is best). Also, if available put on some night sounds on repeat (thunderstorms, sounds of nighttime, or if you want a very shocking experience play *Plague Mass* by Diamanda Galas). If you have an altar, put the candles on the altar with the light one on the right and the dark one on the left. Light the candles and put the black mirror in front of you.

Perform the Kabbalistic Cross in front of the Altar.

- Atoh (above head)
- Io Adonai (at throat)
- Malkut (at feet)
- Ve-Gevurah (right shoulder)
- Ve-Gedulah (left shoulder)
- La-Olam (hands at center)
- Amen (hands folded)

Wrap the cloak or covering around you, covering your head, but leave your face uncovered so you can see the black mirror. Get into a comfortable position.

- Gaze into the black mirror
- Intone – Lilith, Lilith, Lilith
- Say the following:
    - Queen of Night; Mother of Darkness; Goddess of those Abandoned.
    - I come before you as your child, waiting upon your presence.
    - I seek to be your vessel in this world.
    - Cleanse me of my shadow and fill me with your presence.

  - I am Lilin/Lilu (Lilin if you identify as female, Lilu if you identify as male – either or both if you are non-binary); I am yours and you are mine; we are one.

- Chant: Lilith, Lilith, Lilith....

- When you feel connected to her spirit, see Lilith gazing back at you.
- Imagine her hand coming out of the black mirror and touching you. Long pale hands with black talon like nails.
- As soon as she touches you, feel yourself inside the mirror with her for just an instant.
- And then you are back in your body.

Something of you was left inside the mirror. This is your shadow–the part of you which is not truly you. The part of you your ego has created in separation. However, something was replaced. You will perceive a dark presence within. It is not evil, in fact quite the opposite, but it is a spark of Lilith's soul which has taken residence within you. You feel it expanding to fill every part of your body, joining to your spirt. You are now truly Lilith's child, marked by her. You have strength of mind you never knew you could have, and your path is clear as you follow the Dark Mother. Say the following:

- Thank you, my Mother for cleansing me.
- Thank you, my Queen for making me yours.
- As it is spoken, so it is done.

The ritual is complete. You can stop the sounds of night, blow out the candles, and put away the items used for the ritual. You will have incredible dreams over the next few weeks and your life will be changed forever. Situations may not change, but you will have the ability to conquer anything which comes your way.

PART 3
PATHS

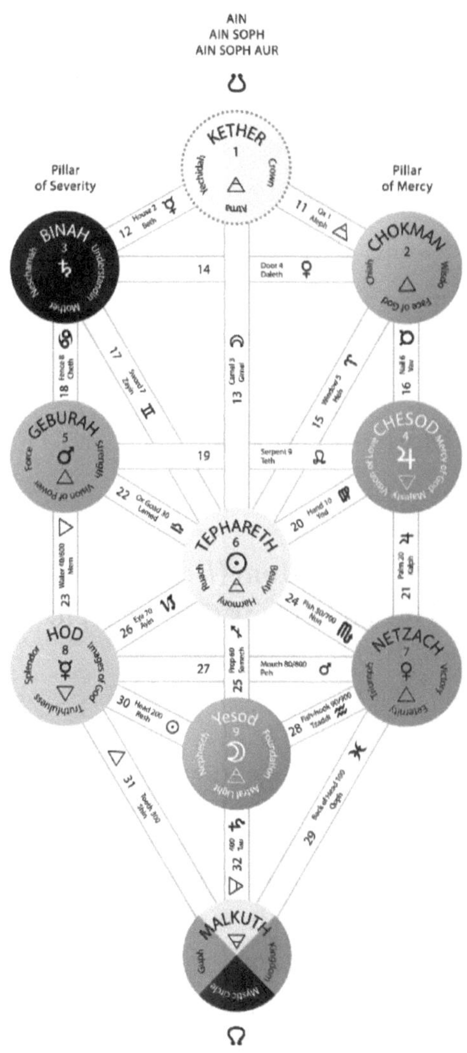
AIN
AIN SOPH
AIN SOPH AUR
KETHER
1
Crown
Pillar
of Severity
Pillar
of Mercy
BINAH
3
Understanding
Mother
CHOKMAN
2
Face of God
12
11
14
Door 4
Daleth
13
17
15
18
16
GEBURAH
5
Force
Strength
Vision of Power
CHESOD
4
Mercy of God
Majesty
19
Serpent 9
Teth
22
20
TEPHARETH
6
Ruach
Beauty
Harmony
23
21
26
24
HOD
8
Splendor
Truthfulness
NETZACH
7
Victory
Eternity
27
25
Mouth 80/800
Peh
30
28
Yesod
9
Foundation
Astral Light
31
32
29
MALKUTH
Guph
Kingdom
Mystic circle

Card: The Fool
Letter: *Aleph* א (Mother letter - air)
Gematria: 1
Key: 0
Path: Crown (*Keter*) to Wisdom (*Hokmah*)
Qlipothic Path: The Twin Gods (*Thaumiel*) to The Hinderers (*Ghagiel*)

The Letter: ***Aleph***

Aleph is the first letter of the Hebrew *Aleph-Bet,* and unlike most letters has no sound. It is the moment before sound manifests. *Aleph*'s literal meaning is "Ox," and it is associated with the Spirit. This may seem a strange combination, but the linkage makes sense once more is understood about the letter.

It is believed the Hebrew written language was created during the age of Taurus, and the Ox or Bull is the symbol of the Taurian age. It is also because an ox is a domesticated animal used to cultivate the land. There is a correlation between our spirit and ego being used to cultivate us just like the ox is used to cultivate the land.

The Hebrew word for the spirit associated with *Aleph* is *Ruach* which is the level of the soul that links our human intelligence with divine intelligence. It is life force and the connection between ego and soul. Interestingly, the actual letter *Aleph* is composed of several of the symbol for the letter *Yod*. *Yod* is associated with God's spirit.

Because it has a numerical value of 1, *Aleph* is also the symbol of unity. Jewish *Midrash* teaches that God told the *Aleph*, "You are one, I am One, and the *Torah* is one." *Aleph* is the letter which begins the names of God: *Ehieh*, *Elohim*, and *Adonai*. It is the first letter of the word *achad* which means one and *ahava* which means love.

Aleph is also the symbol for man, and for firsts in humankind. This is because it is also the first letter of the names of the first man (Adam), the prophet of Messiah (Elijah), and the first Jew (Abraham).

The *Qlipothic* Path: *Aleph*

In the *Qlipoth*, *Aleph* represents divine will creating duality to eventually ensure unity. This path is the eternal void emanating to create the Tree of Shadows. The letter *Aleph* can be divided into three parts, representing the chaos, void, and darkness left over from the previous universe. These components are used to pre-load the current universe with *Qlipothic* forces.

The Tarot Card: The Fool (Key 0)

The Fool is a pictorial representation of the energy of the letter *Aleph*. The key of 0 represents the No Thing (*Ain*) or limitless life energy. The key of 0 also represents the cosmic egg which contains everything needed for growth and development. If you look at the definition for one (*Aleph's* numerical value is 1 vs. the key of 0), it is a beginning. Thus, The Fool is the beginning of a cycle.

The imagery of the card contains a bright white sun with a yellow sky. The white sun is a reference to the pure light of consciousness and then the yellow sky is energy flowing down through the Tree of Life. It is also the Spiritual Sun, which never rises or sets but is ever present, representing universal energy which is radiated from all the stars in the universe. The mountains in the background are the supernal heights, with white mountain peaks suggesting the idea that when it melts, the water feeds the valley below.

The Fool is neither male nor female, but both at once. Him/Her being a youth affirms that the One Force never ages, is always at the height of its power, and has great confidence and joy. The Fool's hair is yellow (radiant energy) and there is a wreath around their head. The green wreath represents the natural divinity of the Fool as Spirit. The wand is will, and the wallet is memory; the rose in his/her hand is white and represents the purified desire of enlightenment.

The Fool's clothes are a white undergarment and a dark outer garment lined in red. The white represents purity, truth, and wisdom, while the dark outer garment represents ignorance and delusion. The red is about passion, desire, and action. The belt around the waist has twelve links, which represent the astrological signs. The seven links visible also stand for the seven lower *Sephirot* (the *Sephirot* of Construction). To break through illusion, the card implies, we must break out of time and space and find the innate consciousness behind all things.

The letters IHVH are shown on the white cloth by the Fool's neck. These represent the Hebrew letters *Yod Heh Vav Heh* (the name of God, *Yahweh*--He Who Was, Is, and Shall Be). There are ten wheels (surrounded by seven trefoils) on the garment, and these wheels have eight spokes. The ten wheels symbolize the ten *Sephirot* of the Tree of Life, and the seven trefoils represent the seven *Sephirot* of Construction (Sphere 1 – 7) which represent creation and our chakras.

As previously stated, the black wand over The Fool's shoulder is will, which links with the wallet, memory. The eye on the wallet is the all-seeing eye and represents our third eye. The white dog is the Fool's ego or personality display. It is white because at this stage it is still pure and tamed (unlike a wild wolf), subordinate to the Spirit.

Meditation With the Fool

Picturing yourself as a Tarot card is an immensely powerful meditative technique which can help you get in touch with the consciousness of the path.

- After performing primordial meditation, picture yourself as the Fool, standing on the side of a cliff with no cares and with non-dual awareness.
- See the white sun in the sky above you with bright yellow atmosphere all around you. This atmosphere is pure light, warming and enlightening you.
- Place your personality into the dog trailing behind. Realize that what is left of you is your true self, pure spirit."
- Abide in this feeling of unity and spirit for as long as you can.
- When finished, bring yourself back to normal awareness and exit the meditation.

Lilith Consciousness

The consciousness of Lilith at this path is Omoroca, the great black dragon of the void. Omoroca is the energy of the Dark Mother beyond time and space who sits on the very tip of *Keter* and *Thaumiel*. She is the *Tzim-Tzum* (restriction) that creates space as the womb of creation; the darkness that is potential for all possibilities. There is little which can be truly grasped of this intelligence while incarnate, because she is so far away from human ideas and concepts.

Lilith Meditation

The purpose of this meditation is to clear the mind, learn to manage thoughts and emotions, and listen--to become one with the emptiness of Lilith beyond creation.

- Turn off all the lights and get into a comfortable position. You need to be in as dark a space as possible.
- Leave your eyes open.
- Push all thoughts aside and begin to breathe in a regular rhythm.
- Breathe in… and out… in… and out
- As thoughts arise, gently push them aside and re-focus on the flame.
- Call on Lilith as Omoroca. Picture the darkness around you as the great dragon of the abyss.
- Feel her all around you, taking up all space.
    - Breathe in… and out… in… and out.
- Abide in this space, communing with the Dark Mother as long as you are able.
- When finished, bring yourself back to normal awareness and end the meditation.

Card: The Magician
Letter: *Bet* ב (Double letter)
Gematria: 2
Key: 1
Path: Crown (*Keter*) to Understanding (*Binah*)
Qlipothic Path: The Twin Gods (*Thaumiel*) to The Concealers (*Satariel*)

The Letter: ***Bet***

The second Hebrew letter is *Bet,* which means "house." The word has a literal meaning "of the ground," which refers to a house needing to be set firmly upon the Earth. *Bet* is a symbol of blessing and creation--duality and plurality. The gematria of 2 represents the concept of duality.

The *Torah* begins with the letter *Bet* instead of *Aleph,* "In the beginning" (*Be-Reshit*). The house of *Bet* is also a focal point for holiness on earth because it can be a Sanctuary or Holy Temple. *Bet* can even be the house of creation because everything in this world contains polarities.

Bet is one of the seven double letters that have two different pronunciations. One pronunciation is hard and the other soft; double letters are always assigned a pair of opposites. *Bet* is the house of both Life and Death.

In the book of Genesis, when Jacob slept in the wilderness, he felt certain he was alone. But when he awoke and struggled with the angel, he learned about *Bet*. So, he named the place *Bet El* (the House of God). God has many houses: *Bet Ha-Midrash* (ancient house of holiness), *Bet Ha-Knesset* (house of meeting and prayer), and *Bet Ha-Midrash* (house of searching and study). *Bet* is the house God visits. So, the world is home for those who remember *El Elyon* (God Most High) built this house.

The *Qlipothic* Path: *Bet*

In the *Qlipoth, Bet* is the house of death and chaos. It is the place of transformation that allows evolution through destruction. *Bet* in the Tree of Life is the house that God lives in. In the *Qlipoth, Bet* is the house that Satan and Moloch inhabit, ensuring the potential to become more than is restricted by the world and our consciousness.

The Tarot Card: The Magician (Key: 1)

The Magician can give us insight into the energy of the letter *Bet*. The card depicts man as the one who directs the force by which he transforms his consciousness and reaches the stage of initiation.

The key number 1 of this card refers to a point of focus. The Magician focuses his concentration on this point, showing humans need to learn to concentrate to perform true magick. There is a famous quote by Arthur C. Clarke which states: "Magic is just science we don't understand yet." Because magick is tied to our world view and our focus, it is a process of building our house using our will and the forces of nature. A person builds his own personal house by developing his higher states of consciousness. The self-conscious states of mind initiate and determine the subconscious reactions.

The roses above the Magician's head are an arbor creating shelter and symbolic of a house (or *Bet*). The red roses represent desire energy that the Magician draws from above and modifies by will. All humans' waking consciousness is motivated by some type of desire.

The infinity symbol (horizontal figure 8) above the Magician's head represents eternity, spirit, and dominion over the physical plane. The Magician's black hair represents ignorance, to which all humans are subject, but the white band around his head means this ignorance is limited by knowledge. His uplifted right hand holding the wand draws down the energy and symbolizes, "That which is below is as that which is above, and that which is above is as that which is below." The fact both ends come to a point shows the duality of all magickal operations–both those leading to higher consciousness and those resulting in works of ego. The left hand pointing down shows the Magician has control over energy he brings down, as well as the forces of the world. His expression of concentration reveals that he knows the secret of being able to control forces below the plane of self-conscious awareness.

The Magician's white inner robe represents the light of perfect wisdom; the snake girdle represents wisdom and eternity in the form of the *ouroboros*; and the red outer garment represents desire, passion, and activity. The red robe is open so it can be slipped off at will, so self-consciousness may enter action or abstain from it, according to circumstances.

The table is his altar, on which he focuses his attention. On the table rest the four symbols of the Tarot suits. They refer to the natural elements of fire (wand), water (cup), air (sword), and earth (coin or pentacle). The objects symbolize the four lower universes of creation and correspond to the letters of Yod Heh Vav Heh. The Magician's Garden is lush and productive, showing that the subconscious plane of mental activity is full of both desire (red roses) and abstract thought untainted by desire (the white lilies).

Meditation With the Magician

Picturing yourself as a Tarot card is an immensely powerful meditative technique which can help you get in touch with the consciousness of the path.

- After performing primordial meditation, picture yourself as the Magician, standing under the arbor.
- You are standing with a wand reaching up and your other hand pointing down. You are a conduit for the energy that is being moved through your will.
- See the table in front of you with the pentacle, wand, cup, and sword. These objects represent the energies of the four universes and of the four elements.
- Feel your will, focus, and energy moving through you from above to below.
- Abide in this feeling of moving energy as long as you can.
- When finished, bring yourself back to normal awareness and end the meditation.

Lilith Consciousness

Lilith's consciousness at this path is as the mistress of evolution, the one who pushes souls toward transformation through the process of life and death. She is the palace of many rooms where we abide in various states of being, moving between dwellings as we move through incarnations and after-life states. In this persona, Lilith is both the beauty and the horror of the universe as she guides us through the joy of birth and the pain of death.

Lilith Meditation

The purpose of this meditation is to clear the mind, learn to manage thoughts and emotions, and listen–to become one with Lilith as the palace of life and death. For this meditation you will need a candle.

- Light the candle, turn off all the lights, and get into a comfortable position.
- Fix your gaze on the candle flame.
- Push all thoughts aside and begin to breathe in a regular rhythm.
    - Breathe in… and out… in… and out
- As thoughts arise, gently push them aside and re-focus on the flame.
- Call on Lilith as Mother Lilith
- As the candle flame flickers, see yourself in your mind's eye, walking through the flame.
- Picture the flame as a doorway.
- After you pass through the flame, breathe in… and out… in… and out.
- Feel your spirit moving between states of being.
- Keep repeating this exercise as many times as you can. If you start to feel your concentration waning, stop the meditation.
- When finished, bring yourself back to normal awareness and exit the meditation.

Card: The High Priestess
Letter: *Gimel* ג (Double letter)
Gematria: 3
Key: 2
Path: Crown (*Keter*) to Beauty (*Tiferet*)
Qlipothic Path: The Twin Gods (*Thaumiel*) to The Disputers (*Thagirion*)

The Letter: *Gimel*

The energy of *Gimel* is like a wave rolling into the world. *Bet* is the place of beginning, but *Gimel* is the act of beginning. According to the teaching of reincarnation, souls return again and again so they may rise to ever higher rungs of the ladder of enlightenment. This is called *Gilgulim*.

As one of the double letters, *Gimel* has both a hard and soft pronunciation. The opposites it connotes are peace and strife. Consider the roles commerce, communication, and transportation play on a global scale and how they relate to peace and war.

Gimel is a cognate of the Hebrew word *Gamol,* which means to nourish until completely ripe. *Gimel* is shaped like a camel, symbolizing travel, commerce, and communication. Because the camel is used for transportation it is known as the "Ship of the Desert." *Gimel* also represents deity's eternal beneficence. Without this divine quality, the world would not exist for even a moment.

Unity is the mode of consciousness attributed to *Gimel* because a camel "brings" distant places together and unites them. Unification is the power of joining things together—connecting pieces, ideas, and people to make a harmonious whole.

The Qlipothic Path: *Gimel*

In the Qlipoth, *Gimel* is the transportation in and out of the Abyss. This force of movement allows for unity of the inner dark suns. This is the path of *Nakash,* the serpent in the Garden, to move up and down through consciousness.

The Tarot Card: The High Priestess (Key: 2)

The title High Priestess means "Chief Female Elder", and is the primary receptive aspect of creation. The High Priestess corresponds to all the virgin goddesses of all traditions and represents Lilith before she realizes her true potential and before she emanates Samael. The veil between the pillars indicates the High Priestess is a virgin, which means she is untouched by whatever happens. She is eternally the same at her core no matter what changes around her.

The High Priestess sits in a temple of Solomon. Her key number is two, representing duplication, reproduction, reflection, and transcription. Two also represents duplicity, untruth, error, and delusion. The subconscious duplicates and repeats the mistakes of faulty, superficial, self-conscious observations. Because the High Priestess holds the *Torah* scroll, she is also the "Keeper of Records" who does not forget anything that transpires.

The walls and her vestments are blue; they represent the moon and water for the creative world and the cosmic mind. The two pillars on either side of the High Priestess are the pillars of Mercy and Severity in the Kabbalistic Tree of Life. They are opposite in color but alike in form, being positive and negative.

The High Priestess herself holds the position of the Middle Pillar, which is the path of equilibrium, compassion, and balance. She is silent, non-judgmental, receptive, non-discriminating, and neutral. The High Priestess' throne is a cube representing the material world or physical manifestation. The High Priestess sits on the cube because the basis of all subconscious mental activity is what has happened and exists, although the interpretation of these facts can be misunderstood by the conscious mind.

The caps of the pillars are lotus buds and represent the latent unrealized power of the virgin High Priestess. The forces of subconsciousness have not yet come into full bloom. The veil contains images of male palms and female pomegranates, suggesting the union of the positive and negative, male and female forces. Compare the arrangement of the pomegranates and the palms with the Tree of Life and the position of the High Priestess corresponding to the path on the Tree from *Keter* to *Tiferet*. This path is the path between physical incarnation and enlightenment.

She holds a scroll marked Tora (*Torah*), and it is her book of memory. It is the subconscious' record of all that has happened. All mental and physical stresses are indelibly impressed on the subconscious–in both the personal and universal sense. As the collective subconscious, it contains the history of all of us throughout all time. Connecting with the collective subconscious is what makes telepathy possible

The water flows out from the High Priestess' robe representing the stream of consciousness. Watch for the water's progress through the other cards.

Meditation With the High Priestess

Picturing yourself as a Tarot card is an immensely powerful meditative technique which can help you get in touch with the consciousness of the path.

- After performing primordial meditation, picture yourself as the High Priestess sitting on her cube throne.
- You are in a temple with a black pillar on the left and a white pillar on the right. There is a fabric tapestry hanging behind you.
- You hold the scroll of knowledge and its mysteries seep into your soul.
- There is a crescent moon below your feet, illuminating you.
- You are clothed in heavy robes, but the robes are turning to liquid and flowing down out of view.
- Abide in this feeling, being bathed in moonlight, having the mysteries of life seep into you, and feel your consciousness residing in you, but also flowing like water into the unknown.
- After a time, feel all the energy return to your form.
- When finished, bring yourself back to normal awareness and exit the meditation.

Lilith Consciousness

The consciousness of Lilith at this path is Eishet Zununim. Eishet is called a whore because she welcomes anyone, turning none away. This is not a slur because our Mother is loving and will take any who are willing to do the work of transformation. As was described in Sphere 0 Da'at, she is also called *Kodeshah,* indicating she is holy and sacred. Lilith on this path can assist one's journey through the abyss, down into creation or back into unification.

Lilith Meditation

This meditation allows us to visualize our energy centers and move energy up and down the central column in our spine while working with Eishet Zununim. This is both a meditation and a chanting exercise.

- Get into a comfortable position.
- Push all thoughts aside and begin to breathe in a regular rhythm.
- Breathe in… and out… in… and out
- As thoughts arise, gently push them aside and re-focus on your breathing.
- Picture your heart filled with light and positive energy–the energy of deity.
- Envision a sphere of brilliant white light, a diamond-like light that sparkles with rainbow hues, translucent and clear, above your head. Visualize and feel this center of supernal light there, above your head. Awaken this center of divine energy with the intonation of the divine name: Omoroca <oh-mo-roc-a>.

- Then envision the light descending through your head down to your throat, forming another sphere of light at your throat, a sphere of translucent lavender light, brightly shining. Awaken this center of divine energy with the intonation of the divine name: Lilith <lil-ith>.
- Let the light continue its descent down through your body to form another sphere of light in the middle of your torso at your solar plexus, a sphere of translucent golden light that shines brightly like the sun. Awaken this divine center with the intonation of the divine name: Eishet Zununim <eye-shet zoo-new-nim>.
- Envision the light naturally and spontaneously continuing its descent, forming another sphere of translucent violet light at your groin, a vibrant and brightly shining center of divine energy. Awaken this divine center with the intonation of the divine name: Lilit <lil-it>.
- Let the light complete its descent, passing down to your feet and forming a sphere of radiant darkness there, as though composed of a radiant indigo or obsidian black translucent light, all receiving. Awaken this divine center of energy with the intonation of the divine name: Na'amah <nay-ah-ma>
- Picture all the spheres glowing bright. Call upon the name of Eishet, asking her for her assistance.
- Picture the lights turning black from the bottom up, starting at your feet and raising all the way to the sphere above your head.
- Feel all the lights in unison, blinking brighter with each breath.

- Feel your consciousness raise to the light above your head. Abide with your thoughts there as long as you are able.
- When this is complete, return to normal consciousness and close the meditation.

Card: The Empress
Letter: *Dalet* ד (Double letter)
Gematria: 4
Key: 3
Path: Wisdom (*Hokmah*) to Understanding (*Binah*)
Qlipothic Path: The Hinderers (*Ghagiel*) to The Concealers (*Satariel*)

The Letter: *Dalet*

The letter *Dalet* contains some of *Bet* (House) and some of *Gimel* (Commerce and Communication) because it is in and out–departure and return. *Dalet* means door, which admits or keeps out. It is what someone or something enters or exits, but it can be locked to keep out (or in) something not permitted to pass. In some texts it is associated with the door of life or the womb.

The consciousness of *Dalet* is around personal safety, self-preservation, and the ability to develop what is useful for us. It also denotes ingress and egress, movement in and movement out. Think about how this relates to the mind and soul, because *Dalet* is the door few people know and even fewer are brave enough to pass through.

The Gematria of *Dalet* is 4, and so there are 4 doors. The first door is *Dahl* (poor) which is a proud door of a poor man's house. The second door is the *Dahm* (blood) put on the lintels of the doors in Egypt where the first born were slain. The next door opens the Ark of the Covenant, because above it is written *Da Lifney Mi Ata Omed Da*: "[Know] before whom you stand. You also stand before the *Dayahn* (Judge)." The last door is devoting yourself to the eternal consciousness — *Devekut*.

The Qlipothic Path: *Dalet*

In the Qlipoth, *Dalet* is the door to chaos. It illuminates through darkness, showing what is hidden. The door opens the ability to traverse the Tree of Shadows to receive the gnosis of the dragon, for either enlightenment or madness.

The Tarot Card: The Empress (Key 3)

The Empress means "she who sits in order." She is the feminine ruling power and consort of the Emperor (the next path). The Empress is the mother goddess in contrast to the High Priestess who is the virgin goddess.

Her key is the number three, which denotes multiplication, development, growth, unfoldment, and therefore expression. The key of three is the understanding of what has been manifested, in contrast to the last path (The High Priestess), which looks back into the self-knowledge of one (I AM). It is through growth that one is able to manifest with the limitless light of *Ain Sof Or* (Eternal Light). This card is the subconscious response to self-conscious suggestion and interpretation, which determines how we act outwardly. Wisdom and folly are the opposites assigned to *Dalet* by Kabbalists.

The occult meanings of *Dalet* points to the subconscious' great power of deductive reasoning. Kabbalists call this luminous intelligence because the subconscious can enlighten us. However, if the subconscious is given false information from the conscious mind, it can create in ignorance by not using all the facts of a situation.

The background of this card shows cypress trees and the foreground ripening wheat because The Empress is Mother Nature. The stream and pool in the background is the "stream" of consciousness, which flows from the High Priestess's robes in the preceding card. The stream falling into the pool is suggestive of the union of male and female modes of cosmic energy.

The Empress' yellow hair symbolizes radiant energy, and the green myrtle in her hair is nature. The meaning here is that reaching the subconscious is reaching nature. Nature can be beautiful and empowering, but it can also be dark and destructive. The Empress wears a crown of twelve stars, meaning she has dominion over the laws of the Zodiac. Beside her sits a heart-shaped shield with the symbol of femininity. Her necklace of pearls relates to phases of the Moon. Her scepter has a globe—showing she has dominion over the physical world (as does our subconscious).

Meditation With the Empress

Picturing yourself as a Tarot card is an immensely powerful meditative technique which can help you get in touch with the consciousness of the path.

- After performing primordial meditation, picture yourself as the Empress sitting on her throne.
- You are in a lush garden with the bright, warm yellow sun shining down on you.
- You can hear the rustling of trees, the sound of water flowing through the stream, and you can smell flowers.
- There is a crown of stars on your head and a scepter in your hand. These are both symbols of divinity, but also physical manifestations of dominion over creation.

- You are clothed in a flowing robe, and you are aware there is life within you. You are pregnant with creation.
- Abide as the Empress, focusing on the creation within. Feel what it's like to manifest from subconscious but focusing on creating from true knowledge.
- After a time, feel all the energy return to your form.
- When finished, bring yourself back to normal awareness and exit the meditation.

Lilith Consciousness

The consciousness of Lilith at this path is that of Obizuth. She is a form of Lilith who is not mentioned other than in the apocryphal Testament of Solomon. Because the references to Obizuth are obscure, there is little known of her other than her complexion has a green tint, her hair is long and snake-like, and her body is hidden in shadow. Obizuth is serpentine and associated with the dragon. She is associated with tormenting women in childbirth; however, she is said to be bright and cheerful. Because childbirth is already painful her purpose is probably less direct than inferred… It is more likely she enters the mind of those giving birth, opening gateways in their psyche to explore possibilities of creation.

Lilith Meditation

This meditation is a way to move energy between yourself and Lilith or between someone else and Lilith.

- Get into a comfortable position.
- Push all thoughts aside and begin to breathe in a regular rhythm.
- Breathe in… and out… in… and out
- As thoughts arise, gently push them aside and re-focus on your breathing.
- Call on Lilith and ask her to fill you with her dark light.
- Picture your heart filled with her dark light and energy.
- As you breathe in, feel your breath coming in and mixing in your heart, energizing you with the dark light of Lilith.
- As you breathe out, feel the breath leaving warmer and filled with Lilith energy.
- Abide in this cleansing until you feel comfortable.
- Picture someone who needs healing, protection, or Lilith's energy (this can be you, a friend, or anyone, including a group of people).
- Picture shadowy cold energy coming from whomever you are giving this energy to.
- Breathe in the shadowy cold energy. When mingling with your heart, it turns warm and fills with Lilith's dark light.
- Breathe out and transmit Lilith's energy to whomever you are practicing for.
- When you feel the process is complete you can return to normal consciousness and end the meditation.

Card: The Emperor
Letter: *Heh* ה (Simple letter)
Gematria: 5
Key: 4
Path: Wisdom (*Hokmah*) to Beauty (*Tiferet*)
Qlipothic Path: The Hinderers (*Ghagiel*) to The Disputers (*Thagirion*)

The Letter: ***Heh***

Heh is used in Hebrew like "the" is used in English. The consciousness of this letter is the defining intelligence. To define something, we must first name it. This associates it with Adam being given the job of naming all the animals in Eden. Our personal definitions of our experiences are accepted by our subconscious, and our perceptions become our realities. We can change our perceptions and our realities, but it requires conscious effort to do so. *Heh* means Window (literally Wind-Door). Consider the function of a window. It is constructed to permit light (knowledge) and air (breath or spirit) to enter the House (*Bet*) of Personality. Windows also allow you to decide whether to admit someone who comes to the door. The Emperor on the Tree of Life connects *Hokmah* to *Tiferet* (Wisdom to Beauty).

Because *Heh* is the sound of breathing out, the sound of *Heh* in every word spoken. God said at the burning bush: "I will be who I will be," (*Ehieh Asher Ehieh*) which contains the letter *Heh* multiple times. In Jewish wedding ceremonies the couple says to each other: "Behold, I will try with all my being to be present for you" (*Haray Aht Miku-Deshet Li)*. There is also *Hu* which means "he," Hua which means "she," and then *Haym* which means "them."

The *Qlipothic* Path: *Heh*

In the *Qlipoth, Heh* is the window of spirit, so what is concealed can be seen and heard. The structures of society and consciousness, which can either be used or need to be dismantled, are seen and understood. This allows for the undoing of that which does not serve, liberating us.

The Tarot Card: The Emperor (Key 4)

The title for The Emperor is "He who sets in order" –it implies both authority and paternity. This is related to the Empress, whose title is "She who sits in order." It also signifies the head of government, the source of war, etc. The Zodiac sign attributed to this card is Aries (War) –a sun sign.

The Emperor's crown is ringed with 12 triangles, reminding us of the Empress' crown of 12 stars. Consider that a window allows you to see out of the house, and sight is attributed to the Emperor. The organ of sight is the eye, often called the window to the soul. The consciousness attributed to *Heh* is to constitute; to frame; to compose. It is also related to authorship and connected to paternity. The key number four is about order, measurement, classification, recording and tabulation.

The mountains in the background are severe in contrast to the valley the Empress sits in. They represent the potential for sterility of supervision and regulation. On the other hand, it is the erosion of these rocks which provides the soil for the valley of the Empress' garden. Below the base of the mountains is a river; this is the same flow of consciousness as in the other cards. The ram's head on the throne represent Aries, Mars, and war. The Emperor sits on a throne because he is the master of framing realty.

His robe is purple, identifying him as royalty, and his undergarment is red for passion. Even though the Emperor has the color of passion, his armor shows that he is stiff and set in his ways. His scepter is a form of the Egyptian Ankh (sign of life) which has a T-square on it, representing geometry and math as well as the letter *Tav*. The power of regulation can set us free from slavery and circumstance. In his other hand is the globe, a typical symbol of dominion.

The Emperor is an old man with a white beard, representing the Ancient of Days (from the Bible and Kabbalah). The Emperor is the consort of the Empress, and he is who the Magician becomes after fathering the Empress' children. After becoming a father, he can exercise his paternal authority.

Psychologically, therefore, he represents the self-consciousness of a person. He is the lawgiver or regulator who creates the framework of one's personal world.

Meditation With the Emperor

Picturing yourself as a Tarot card is an immensely powerful meditative technique which can help you get in touch with the consciousness of the path.

- After performing primordial meditation, picture yourself as the Emperor sitting on his thrown.
- You are outside in a stark and craggy land. There are mountains in the distance and a small stream behind you.
- You can hear the whistling of the wind and the sound of water flowing through the stream.

- There is a crown on your head, and you are holding a scepter in your right hand and a globe in your left.
- You are clothed in royal robes and armor.
- You are an older man with white hair and a long beard.
- Abide as the Emperor. As you gaze out at your surroundings, you know you are the one who makes the rules for the kingdom, taking sensory input and making a framework for life.
- When finished, bring yourself back to normal awareness and exit the meditation.

Lilith Consciousness

Lilith consciousness at this path is in her power of transformation. She is the window which allows sights and sounds to pass from our unconscious mind to our conscious mind and back again. The human mind let's all pass back and forth with no power or control over what is transmitted. Through meditation and the power of Lilith, we can refine what is passed back and forth, changing our world view and our very essence.

Lilith Meditation

The Silent Witness is a meditation we explored earlier in this book. This time we are going to practice it more fully with Lilith.

- Get into a comfortable position.

- Push all thoughts aside and begin to breathe in a regular rhythm.
- Breathe in… and out… in… and out
- As thoughts arise, gently push them aside and re-focus on your breathing.
- Call on Lilith to empower you and to be the lens of your mind, through which you witness events.
- Let your mind wander to the events of the day.
- Recall anything that went well or poorly. Set aside your judgment and let Lilith look at these events.
- As you breathe in, feel her analyzing what has transpired.
- As you breathe out, feel her speaking of what needs to be transformed. This is not judgment, but refinement.
- Abide in this state, repeating the process until there are no more events to review.
- When this is complete, you can return to normal consciousness and close the meditation.

Card: The Hierophant
Letter: *Vav* ו (Simple letter)
Gematria: 6
Key: 5
Path: Wisdom (*Hokmah*) to Mercy (*Hesed*)
Qlipothic Path: The Hinderers (*Ghagiel*) to The Smiters (*Gha'ag Sheblah*)

The Letter: *Vav*

Vav means nail or hook and is thus something to hang other things on. Because other things depend on it, it is a means of union—a means of support. *Vav* conveys binding things together, linking them, and is related to aid or assistance. *Vav* is like the English word "and," literally joining words together. The Hierophant connects *Hokmah* to *Hesed,* Wisdom to Mercy. The central thought of this card is union.

In Sanskrit yoga means "union" and is like the Hebrew letter *Vav*. Yoga is also the root of our word "yoke." The physical and spiritual discipline of *yoga* is a system in which the personal consciousness is directly linked to the universal consciousness. Its object is direct, first-hand connection to the Universal conscious energy. This experience is considered natural though rare. The Hierophant is the mode of consciousness in effect when these types of experiences occur.

Vav is the sound of being joined. We read: "And you will eat. And you will be satisfied. And you will thank God." People, ideas, and actions are real because they are separate one from another, being unique. Only something which is unique can be joined to something else. The only Hebrew word to begin with *Vav* is confession (*Vi-Dui*).

Eternal intelligence is the mode of consciousness corresponding with *Vav*. It gives assurance of the ultimate triumph of the life power, which is eternal, carrying with it the conviction of immortality. The Inner Voice gives us solutions to problems by applying those principles which we recognize as true yesterday, today, and forever. Hearing is the sense attributed to *Vav,* because it links man to man by speech and man to God, through this Inner Voice.

The *Qlipothic* Path: *Vav*

In the Qlipoth, *Vav* is the nail which holds silence so the creative word may be unheard. It shakes loose the firmament and recreates structures, loosening the hold of the material universe in favor of the dark Tree. Reality is unhinged and peeled back to reveal its inner truths.

The Tarot Card: The Hierophant (Key 5)

The Sanskrit noun *"sruti"* means to hear, and it is also the word for revelation. Knowledge of the higher realms of reality comes to us through an inner voice. Hierophant means "revealer of sacred things," although some decks call this card "The Pope." This is not to be associated too closely with the Catholic Pope, but the word pope does mean father.

The path of this card is between *Hokmah* and *Hesed*. *Hokmah* is *Abba* or Father, and *Hesed* is Mercy. The Hierophant could be considered the spiritual parent regardless of gender, being the bridge-maker who links our outer experience and our inner illumination. The key number five represents the dynamic law proceeding from abstract order, and it is associated with versatility.

Much of the coloring of this card is grey to show the balance of opposites, including the two pillars he sits between and the stone chair he sits upon. Stone in Hebrew is spelled *ABN*— *AB* means Father also, and *BN* means Son showing union between what is outside and what is inside creation.

The Hierophant's outer robe is red orange, representing the material world, and the inner white garment stands for enlightenment. His crown is a triple tiara of gold, symbolizing wisdom with three layers representing the creative, formative, and material worlds.

He is holding a golden staff, symbolizing his dominion of the life power throughout creation. The two monks standing before him look identical except for their clothes. The one on the right wears a garment of lilies for purity and rebirth, while the one on the left wears a garment of roses for passion. The Hierophant stands for intuition, which follows reasoning and then adds to it.

Meditation With the Hierophant

Picturing yourself as the Tarot card is an immensely powerful meditative technique which can help you get in touch with the consciousness of the path.

- After performing primordial meditation, picture yourself as the Hierophant sitting on his throne.
- There are two grey pillars on either side of you and a grey throne supporting you. You are wearing a long, loose robe of red with a white inner robe.
- You can feel a large, heavy crown on your head. This crown is the weight of the creative, formative, and material world.

- You hold a staff in your left hand which represents dominion, and your right hand forms the sign of a blessing.
- Two monks stand before you. You realize both are aspects of your personality.
- The one to your left wears a garment with lilies on it. This part of yourself is purity and mercy.
- The one to your right wears a garment with roses on it. This part of yourself is passion and emotion.
- You also realize you need to be the balance of the two aspects… bringing purity, mercy, passion, and emotion together into balance.
- Feel their energy mixing in you and finding a state of equilibrium. When this occurs, energy pours out of your staff, and you begin to channel the power of eternity into the world.
- Abide in this state for a time.
- When finished, bring yourself back to normal awareness and exit the meditation.

Lilith Consciousness

Lilith consciousness at this level is *Belqis,* the Queen of Sheba. As *Belqis,* Lilith is a great African queen. She has power and wealth, yet she seeks the mysteries of creation. The Queen of Sheba makes the journey to Jerusalem to encounter Solomon. She comes to ask him "hard questions." These are not questions about commerce or kingship, but questions of an occult nature. She is a trickster who questions much as the

Sphynx does, for the purpose of revealing truth. She can come to us and reveal our truths and falsehoods if we let her.

Lilith Meditation

The soul vision practice is a visual meditation in which the seeker can get a glimpse of their true nature. This is done through primordial meditation focused on an image of themselves until their third eye, directed by Lilith, sees what is beneath the flesh and blood. For this practice you will need a black mirror. If one is not available, you can substitute a regular mirror.

- Turn off or lower the lights, so there is only minimal light in the room.
- Get into a comfortable position.
- Push all thoughts aside and begin to breathe in a regular rhythm.
- Breathe in… and out… in… and out
- As thoughts arise, gently push them aside and refocus on your breathing.
- Call upon Lilith in the guise of Belqis, the Queen of Sheba. Ask her to give you the ability to view and discern.
- Gaze into the black mirror and see your reflection.
- Continue to breathe in and out focusing on your image.
- Try not to let any thoughts into your awareness, but if they come, push them gently aside.

- Try not to look away from your reflection. You can blink as needed.
- After a time, the image will blur, and you will begin to see changes to your features.
- Take note of what you see without becoming fixated on any specific attributes.
- When you are finished, return to normal consciousness and as soon as possible, write down what you experienced.

Card: The Lovers
Letter: *Zayin* ז (Simple letter)
Gematria: 7
Key: 6
Path: Understanding (*Binah*) to Beauty (*Tiferet*)
Qlipothic Path: The Concealers (*Satariel*) to The Disputers (*Thagirion*)

The Letter: *Zayin*

Zayin means "sword" or "weapon." It is the opposite of *Vav,* the nail because a sword cleaves, cuts, divides, separates. It has two edges, symbolizing life's many possibilities, decisions, and consequences. *Zayin* represents the ability to make fine distinctions; to reach viable and correct conclusions and decisions.

When you do not wield the sword of discrimination and distinction to make your own decisions, those decisions will be made for you and may be less desirable than the decision you would have chosen. *Zayin* is masculine (*Zachar*), and it starts the first letter of the word for beard (*Zakan*). Other words starting with the letter *Zayin* are *old* (*Zakayn*), *time* (*Z'man*), and *remembers* (*Zachaer*). Because *Zayin* is part of memory, it also belongs to the word *Zohar*, The Book of Light. And finally, *Zayin* is the seed (*Zera*).

Disposing Intelligence is the mode of consciousness attributed to *Zayin* and the Lovers. To "dispose" is literally to place apart or to arrange, to distribute, or to divide. This also relates to our disposition or emotional state. Keen perception and discernment are also attributes of Zayin.

The *Qlipothic* Path: *Zayin*

In the *Qlipoth*, *Zayin* is the sword of the dragon that creates duality. It is the force which opens the womb to birth the two headed serpents of opposition. It is also the sacrificial knife used in splitting one's essence to create tension, which leads to opportunity.

The Tarot Card: The Lovers (Key 6)

In the much older versions of Tarot, there are three figures on the Lovers card—a child, a maiden, and a crowned woman. These figures represent the Kabbalistic Son and Bride and the

Great Mother and is a reference to marriage. The title intimates the union of opposites as complementary modes of consciousness.

The key number six is about balance, equilibrium, symmetry, harmony, and reciprocity. The sun in the image is again the great light-source, the energy which infuses all life. Here it is yellow, not white, indicating life and energy but also ageless wisdom.

The Angel is Raphael, angel of air. His violet garments also represent air, since violet is the compliment of yellow. He is the super-consciousness and is thus related to the Fool. The mountains can be seen as the habitat of the Gods, and as a metaphor of the great work of enlightenment. They are the peaks we all must climb on our journey toward the goal.

The man is Adam—the namer of things. He is also the Magician and the Emperor. There is a tree with flaming fruit behind him. This fruit symbolizes the twelve signs of the zodiac. Thus, the tree is a tree of human life in all twelve types. The woman is Eve. She is also the High Priestess and the Empress. Behind her is the Tree of Knowledge of Good and Evil. It bears five fruits—the five senses. Up the tree rises the serpent of sensation. This is because temptation arises from sensation and our grasping at it. The serpent also represents wisdom and redemption. This is because wisdom and liberation come from the right application of these forces which at first tempt us. The man (self-consciousness) looks toward the woman, who (subconsciousness) looks toward the angel (super-consciousness). Self-consciousness is not directly aware of the super-consciousness; it is the subconscious which is aware of the superconscious. This means that we must join our conscious mind to our sub-conscious mind to be able to access the intelligence of the superconscious.

Health, happiness, and well-being depend on the cooperation of these two modes of being. The relationship between self-consciousness and subconscious should be loving intimacy. Note the two figures are nude; they hide nothing from each other. If we want the subconscious to work on our behalf, we must treat it lovingly and not try to bully it, because bullying yields the opposite result. Self-consciousness is the framer of suggestion.

Meditation With the Lovers

Picturing yourself as the Tarot card is an immensely powerful meditative technique which can help you get in touch with the consciousness of the path.

- After performing primordial meditation, picture yourself as the man in the Lovers card.
- You can feel the warmth of the sun beaming down on you. You can hear a soft breeze and smell flowers.
- Behind you is a tree with twelve burning fruit. This represents you as an avatar for all types of people.
- You are looking across to your right and you see a woman. She is your partner. Behind her is the tree of

knowledge of good and evil with five fruit to symbolize the senses.

- You realize you transmit your thoughts and emotions to the woman with your gaze. Messages from her mind begin to flow back to you and become your thoughts as well.
- After you abide in this communication for a time, shift your consciousness to the woman's perceptions. You feel the sun beaming down on you. You can also hear a soft breeze and smell flowers.
- You are looking up at a beautiful angel, Raphael, who is floating in the sky between you and the man.
- You can sense the thoughts and emotions of the man as they flow into you. In turn you send thoughts back to him. You can also feel your thoughts being transmitted to the angel, and visions come from her to you.
- After you abide in the woman's perspective for a time, shift your consciousness to that of the angel. You are one with the Source, unafraid and unchanged by anything happening around you.
- You can sense the thoughts of the man, passing through the woman and being added to by her, as they are transmitted to you.
- You take the messages from the Source which are sparked by the man and woman's thoughts. You transmit these to the woman, and then she transmits them to the man.
- You realize the transmission loses energy and detail as it moves back through the chain, but this is as it is

supposed to be. The man will take what he can and use it for his good.

- After you abide as the angel for a time, you feel your consciousness shift back to the woman and then back to the man.
- When finished, bring yourself back to normal awareness and exit the meditation.

Lilith Consciousness

In this path, Lilith's consciousness is the movement between Lilith the Elder and Norea. Lilith the Elder is Lilith's soul outside of time and space as the great Dark Mother. Norea, the name Na'amah in Coptic, is an incarnate, enlightened being who encounters Noah and his ark. Lilith the Elder is in the supernal realm, while Norea is in creation; however, they share consciousness. This is enlightenment, existence as a being who is incarnate yet connected to their higher self.

Lilith Meditation

This practice is done to assist our subconscious in its connection with the consciousness of that aspect of Lilith which is beyond time and space.

- Get into a comfortable position.
- Push all thoughts aside and begin to breathe in a regular rhythm.
- Breathe in… and out… in… and out.

- As thoughts arise, gently push them aside and refocus on your breathing.
- Call on Lilith, asking her to protect you and open you to vision.
- When you have reached a state of calm, picture yourself floating in a black sea of light.
- There is no beginning and there is no end.
- You realize that the dark water is flowing through your body, and that you have become one with the tides of this great ocean that is Lilith's consciousness.
- Continue to breathe in and out, pushing all other thoughts aside.
- Open up your awareness and let messages from outside you enter. These may be words, pictures, emotions.
- Take note of what you see, feel, and hear without getting to focused on any one detail.
- When you are finished, return to normal consciousness and as soon as possible, write down what you experienced.

Card: The Chariot
Letter: *Chet* ח (Single letter)
Gematria: 8
Key: 7
Path: Understanding (*Binah*) to Severity (*Gevurah*)
Qlipothic Path: The Concealers (*Satariel*) to The Flaming Ones (*Golachab*)

The Letter: ***Chet***

In the *Torah, Chet* is written with a sharp, jagged notch on its top as if it were really two separate letters just touching. However, they need each other to stand. *Chet* is the agony of a soul torn apart from itself. Words beginning with *Chet* are: *Chait* - which is sin (or missing the mark) - a soul torn apart from its true self; *Chasid*–pious one; *Chavel*–pangs of childbirth; *Chayim*–is the word for life which is a seeming separation; Chilul–desecration or breaking sanctity, which drives souls apart; *Chavurah*–a small group may be separate people, but they are joined to accomplish a task; *Churban*–destruction or devastation which seems to be the end; *Chuppa*–the marriage canopy which is a shelter protecting this new joining.

The letter *Chet* means a field and the fence enclosing it. This is a cultivated field as opposed to the open country in Key 6. This is what happens in consciousness when we define something. Speech is attributed to *Chet,* and this indicates that words have protective and preservative powers; thus, using words properly is a means of safety. The consciousness of this letter is an enclosure which defines. In the human personality, forces flow into the personality from outside consciousness. This indicates our thoughts and speech are based in our subconscious.

The *Qlipothic* Path: *Chet*

In the *Qlipoth, Chet* is both the closed fence which is required to allow cultivation, and the open fence when its boarders are no longer needed and would stifle growth. It is the duality of both protection and freedom. This enclosure holds both the dark waters and the dark fire of the Tree of Shadows.

The Tarot Card: The Chariot (Key 7)

The chariot represents enclosure, protection, defense, a specific location, or an area set apart for cultivation. This is about making yourself King or Queen of your circumstances as a natural consequence of your triumphs.

The number seven has many mystical meanings and exploring them could comprise an entire book. The Bible has many references to this number, because many of the books of the Bible were written on a plan of sevens–seven chapters, seven subdivisions, etc. Seven relates to rest, safety, security, and victory. It also represents a temporary cessation, not final perfection.

In the background is a walled city, which equates to a stone fence. There are trees and a river visible in this card to remind us of the symbolism of Key 3, the Empress. This is because speech is not only composed of definitions, but also embodies mental imagery and gives form to the stream of consciousness.

The cards build on each other to tell a story. The river rises from the watery substance of the robe of the High Priestess, and trees are associated with the fertility of the Empress' Garden. The chariot is a movable fence in the shape of a cube, and its grey color symbolizes wisdom and the union of father and son. Above the chariot are four pillars supporting a starry canopy. The number four means order and measurement, as well as the four elements of air, fire, earth, and water. The pillars are divided in half and represent the saying, "That which is above is as that which is below." The canopy represents celestial forces and their descent into the physical reality.

The red symbol on the shield is a Hindu representation of the male-female unity called a *lingam* and *yoni*. The winged globe above the shield represents aspiration. The crown, the color of the man's hair, the lunar crescents, his body armor, belt and skirt, and the scepter he is holding all show that the charioteer is the sum of all the characters which have preceded him in the previous cards. He is the true Self, the source and power of all forms of life-expression. The chariot and canopy symbolize the combination of celestial and terrestrial forces. The sphinxes are a representation of the pillars of mercy and severity.

Meditation With the Charioteer

Picturing yourself as the Tarot card is an immensely powerful meditative technique which can help you get in touch with the consciousness of the path.

- After performing primordial meditation, picture yourself in the chariot.
- You can see the yellow sky and feel the gentle bumps as your chariot moves across the ground.
- You are being pulled by two sphinxes. These are beings of spirit who embody mercy and severity. Because you are being pulled by both, everything is in balance.

- Look up and see the starry sky is your canopy. The stars are the connection to the place of the super-conscious which shines down on you.
- You are completely protected, and no outside energies can enter your chariot. Nothing can derail you from your path.
- When finished, bring yourself back to normal awareness and exit the meditation.

Lilith Consciousness

Consciousness of Lilith at this path is the consciousness of Agrat bat Mahlat. Agrat is one of the most severe forms of Lilith. Because Agrat has been associated with such severity, she is a strong force of protection from both internal and external attacks. In this form Lilith is completely sovereign, doing whatever she likes in whatever fashion she chooses.

Lilith Meditation

This practice is done to create a spiritual shield around us using the power of Lilith. It protects our thoughts and mind from external forces. The point of this exercise is to block any negative energy and focus only on that energy which comes from higher realms.

- Get into a comfortable position.
- Push all thoughts aside and begin to breathe in a regular rhythm.

- Breathe in… and out… in… and out.
- As thoughts arise, gently push them aside and refocus on your breathing.
- When you have reached a state of calm, picture yourself floating in darkness.
- There is no beginning and there is no end.
- Call upon Lilith in the form of Agrat bat Mahlat.
- As you float in this darkness, feel Agrat encircle you with her dark wings, creating an enclosure around you of dark light. This enclosure is a Merkavah–a spiritual chariot. It fully encloses you and is mobile because of its energetic quality.
- Your chariot is solid and impenetrable. The only who can connect with you is Lilith.
- Picture the chariot being so solid that it cannot be destroyed and your place in it is secure. The chariot is always with you.
- Abide in the chariot for a time.
- When you are finished, return to normal consciousness knowing that your mind and body are shielded from any harm.

Card: Strength
Letter: *Tet* ט (Single letter)
Gematria: 9
Key: 8
Path: Mercy (*Hesed*) to Severity (*Gevurah*)
Qlipothic Path: The Smiters (*Gha'ag Sheblah*) to The Flaming Ones (*Golachab*)

The Letter: ***Tet***

One cannot pronounce the letter *Tet* until he or she sees the dew (*Tal*) in the morning. Only when one secretly confesses, he does not understand how the droplets of water have formed can one be cleansed in them. One can then wrap herself in her prayer shawl (*Tallit*). Dew and rain are the water sustaining life (*Tal U'Matar*). One dips oneself (*T'Velah*) and washes off the defilement (*Tum-Ah*) which encrusts the soul. Then one will again find purity (*Tahara*). For *Tet* is good (*Tov*).

Tet means "snake," which is known to occultists as serpent power (kundalini). It is cosmic electricity, the universal life-principle, and the conscious energy in all things. The serpent also represents secrecy, subtlety, and wisdom. This power is "the tempter" in Genesis, and when this force is overcome, it is the means to salvation. The ancients saw the snake shed its skin, so to them it symbolized reincarnation and rebirth. *Tet* is associated with digestion and is symbolized by the *Ouroboros* (the snake eating its own tail). This stands for the cycle of life and immortality, which is self-sustaining. Intelligence of All Spiritual Activity and Secret Works is the mode of consciousness attributed to *Tet*. Remember that all things are spiritual.

The *Qlipothic* Path: *Tet*

In the *Qlipoth, Tet* is the serpent of flame created by sexual polarity. This is the reflection of *Nakash,* the serpent from the Garden, coiled in the form of an *ouroboros* eternally fueling itself. This flaming serpent penetrates anything it can to cause transformation in any form necessary, breaking restrictive and limiting thoughts.

The Tarot Card: Strength (Key 8)

The key number eight represents rhythm, alternate cycles of involution and evolution. It also represents the idea that opposite forms of expression are the effects of a single cause. The card alludes to the fiery life power which is the source of all human action.

The scene in this card is an uninhabited plain. This is to show it is apart from human habitation. The woman's yellow hair identifies her with the Empress, so we may identify her with creative subconscious generation of mental imagery. Instead of a wreath, she wears a crown of flowers. This means the organic process is closer to completion in this card. The horizontal 8 (infinity) appears over her head as it did with the Magician, which means something of the Magician has been transferred to the woman. It shows that the subconscious is affected and altered by self-conscious mental states.

The white, unadorned gown the woman wears symbolizes purity. Since this is the color of *Keter* (the Crown of the Tree of Life) it represents pure spiritual influence from the super-conscious. She wears a belt of roses twisted into another figure 8 (infinity), and she leads the lion with this chain of flowers. It signifies that when we weave our intentions, we can do wonderful things.

The lion, as king of beasts, represents all subhuman forces including ego. The woman tames the lion and opens its mouth, making it articulate. This brings it into humanity, symbolizing that the subconscious is in control of all subhuman manifestations of cosmic energy.

Meditation With Strength

Picturing yourself as the Tarot card is an immensely powerful meditative technique which can help you get in touch with the consciousness of the path.

- After performing primordial meditation, picture yourself as the woman standing on the plain.
- You can see the yellow sky and feel yourself clothed in a simple white robe. There is a wreath of flowers in your hair.
- You are bent over a giant red lion. You are holding its jaws open. and another wreath around your waist is also wrapped around the lion, joining the animal to you.
- You have no fear because the lion is tamed and connected.
- You realize you and the lion are one. Your aspect as the woman is your higher self, and the lion is your ego.
- Abide knowing you and your ego are one. When you think or speak, the lion also speaks, because you are one.
- When finished, bring yourself back to normal awareness and exit the meditation.

Lilith Consciousness

At this level, Lilith is the serpent. She is a great serpent queen (Az) who has mastered the void and blended all duality within herself. In this form she slithers through consciousness and materiality with ease. Her touch is transformation, and her breath is desire brought into its full power. To her, everything can be used for enlightenment and liberation if brought under her control.

Lilith Meditation

Taming the ego (or lower soul/*Nefesh*) is done to create a spiritual link to it. The ego is necessary and useful while one is in a body, but it needs to be connected to the higher self and listening to it. This relevant practice will start with a middle pillar meditation but will continue from there.

- Get into a comfortable position.
- Push all thoughts aside and begin to breathe in a regular rhythm.
- Breathe in… and out… in… and out
- As thoughts arise, gently push them aside and refocus on your breathing.
- Picture your heart filled with light and positive energy–the energy of deity.
- Envision a sphere of brilliant white light, a diamond-like light that sparkles with rainbow hues, translucent and clear, above your head. Visualize and feel this center of supernal light and awaken this center of

divine energy with the intonation of the divine name: *Omoroca* <oh-mo-roc-a>.

- Then envision the light descending through your head down to your throat, forming another sphere of light at your throat. This sphere is translucent lavender light, brightly shining. Awaken this center of divine energy with the intonation of the divine name: Lilith <lil-ith>.
- Let the light continue its descent down through your body to form another sphere of light in the middle of your torso at your solar plexus, a sphere of translucent golden light that shines brightly like the sun. Awaken this divine center with the intonation of the divine name: Norea <nor-e-a>.
- Envision the light naturally and spontaneously continuing its descent, forming another sphere of translucent violet light at your groin, a vibrant and brightly shining center of divine energy. Awaken this divine center with the intonation of the divine name: Lilit <Lil-it>.
- Let the light complete its descent, passing down to your feet and forming a sphere of radiant darkness there. This darkness is an illumined indigo or obsidian black translucent light, all receiving. Awaken this divine center of energy with the intonation of the divine name: Na'amah <nay-ah-ma>
- Having brought Lilith's consciousness down into the body, envision and feel her awakening in your body and soul.
- See your entire body filled with a dark purple glow of Lilith's consciousness.

- Call on Lilith and chant her name several times–Lilith, Lilith, Lilith.
- Picture your ego inside of you as a roaring red beast. Attribute to it selfishness, shortsightedness, and volatility. This is the part of you, which is not truly *you*, but the part that has been created to protect against imagined or real pain.
- Picture the purple light flowing into the beast, taking control of it. The beast slowly gets darker and darker until it is black and serpentine. It ceases to roar.
- Feel the beast stop dominating you. Instead, you are the master of the beast. It is now your true protection, under your will through the power of Lilith.
- Once you feel the beast has been mastered, return to normal consciousness, and end the meditation.

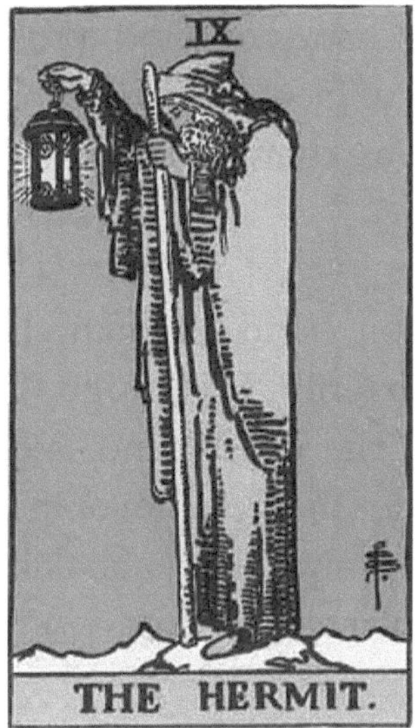

Card: The Hermit
Letter: *Yod* י (Single letter)
Gematria: 10
Key: 9
Path: Mercy (*Hesed*) to Beauty (*Tiferet*)
Qlipothic Path: The Smiters (*Gha'ag Sheblah*) to The Disputers (*Thagirion*)

The Letter: ***Yod***

Yod is the smallest letter and most often represents *Yahweh* or divine spirit. A dove (*Yonah*) starts with the letter *Yod*. The *Yod* participates in the upper worlds—Jerusalem (*Yerushalyim*), God's heavenly city. It also resides in the lower worlds—the inclination of a person toward evil (*Yetzer*). The *Yod* brings them both together in unification (*Yichud*)--the joining of the upper and lower worlds. *Yod* is the hand of God (*Yad Chazaka*). The *Yod* is all which remained of Jacob (*Yakov*) after he wrestled with God and his name was changed to Israel (*Yisra-Ael*).

Yod's literal meaning is the open hand of man. It indicates power, direction, skill, and dexterity. It is a sign of inclination rather than actual activity. The open hand is a beneficial symbol worldwide and indicates the freedom of the Supreme Spirit. *Yod* has special significance in Kabbalah because it is the first letter of the Tetragrammaton (*Yahweh*).

Esoterically, the letter *Yod* corresponds to the experience of union with the true self (and with the consciousness of deity). This experience is compared by occult writers to the ecstasy of sex and what scripture calls "Heaven."

The *Qlipothic* Path: *Yod*

In the *Qlipoth, Yod* is the hand of darkness that breaks the limitations that are put on a soul by karma and destiny. Because *Yod* is the seed that composes the rest of the letters, it is also the force that can rewrite them into new configurations. In the *Qlipoth,* this letter breaks everything that binds to create new, liberating patterns.

The Tarot Card: The Hermit (Key 9)

The Hermit is a title referring to a passage in Kabbalah which says "*Yod* is above all, and with Him is none other associated." This represents the Father who is a hermit and lives alone, isolated. The picture shows the Hermit solitary on a snowy mountain peak. He is high above any other travelers, holding his lantern as a beacon. His white beard helps identify him as the "Ancient One."

His grey robe suggests another Kabbalistic title for the One, "Concealed with all concealment." He is the Source of All, yet he is also the goal of all endeavors. Every practice aims at the union of personal consciousness with the super-consciousness.

Because key 9 represents completion, look at the analogy between 0—The Fool and 9—the Hermit. Nine represents the unity as the goal of existence while 0 represents the same unity as the Source of all. Thus, the Fool is a youth, and the Hermit is a bearded ancient. The Hermit stands in darkness because this consciousness is what is behind our personifications of deity—the reality of deity is darkly incomprehensible to our intellects. The peak he stands on is snow-capped, because to us the Ancient One is an abstraction, cold and far-removed from the warmth of everyday life. He carries his own light for the benefit of any who are trying to reach Him.

The light is a golden hexagram symbolizing union. Even though the Hermit appears to be alone, he is lighting the path for the multitudes below. He has no need to climb, so the staff is in his left hand and is a tool of the Magician. The Hermit is the super-consciousness, the cosmic, eternal urge to freedom. Psychologically, this is the state of being conscious where all will is universal, rather than personal.

Meditation With the Hermit

Picturing yourself as the Tarot card is an immensely powerful meditative technique which can help you get in touch with the consciousness of the path.

- After performing primordial meditation, picture yourself as the Hermit, standing on the cliff.
- It is twilight and although you are in a cold, snowy land, you are not cold because of your heavy robes.
- In your right hand you hold a lantern that shows light in the form of a six-pointed star. Its brightness casts shadows all over the dark landscape.
- In your left hand you hold a staff, which is set on the ground and pointing up above your head.
- Look down into the valley and see your body sitting in meditation.
- Your light shines on your own physical form, illuminating your head with the light of super consciousness.
- The staff brings energy from the higher realms and transfers it to your body in the physical world.
- Abide as this presence as long as you can.

- When finished, bring yourself back to normal awareness and exit the meditation.

Lilith Consciousness

On this path, Lilith's consciousness is focused on breaking limitations and healing. If you are familiar with her myth cycle, you know she is a being who has experienced great trauma, and she has been treated horribly. She is the mother of all who are marginalized, and she will bring great strength and compassion to us on our road to transformation.

Lilith Meditation

Warning – this practice is extremely intense, and I would not recommend it until you have done the work of all the Spheres and all the meditations up to this point.

The Path of Anguish is a transformational journey using Lilith as your guide. Before you begin the practice, have four difficult events from your life in mind, going backward from the most recent to the most distant. The four most difficult events are best, but if there is something you find too painful to recall, use a different memory at this time. You can perform the Path of Anguish again for more difficult events later if you need to.

For this practice you will need a 7-day devotional candle (any color, although red or black would be best). Print out a picture of Lilith and tape it to the glass. You will also need a piece of paper divided into four pieces, a pen, and either a small cauldron or a fire-resistant bowl.

If you have an altar, put the candle, the cauldron, the four pieces of paper, and the pen on the altar. If not, just set up a small table and place these items on it.

Perform the Kabbalistic Cross in front of the Altar.

- Atoh (above head)
- Io Adonai (at throat)
- Malkut (at feet)
- Ve-Gevurah (right shoulder)
- Ve-Gedulah (left shoulder)
- La-Olam (hands at center)
- Amen (hands folded)

Light the candle and say, "Lilith, Mother, I come to you and ask you to protect and strengthen me as I walk the path of anguish".

Take the slips of paper and write down one of the four events from your life that you will be working with in this practice on each one.

Number the slips from one to four, with one being the most recent and four being the one furthest in the past.

Pick up the paper numbered one and hold it between your hands. Think about the event in as much or little detail as you feel you need. If you feel emotional, do not be afraid to cry or feel anger.

State, "Lilith I give this event to you. I trust you to turn it into strength and power for my journey."

When you feel ready, touch the tip of the paper to the flame in the candle. Put the burning paper into the cauldron and say, "As this paper burns, so does my pain."

When the paper has become ash, feel the smoke rise from the cauldron and enter your heart. You feel darkness and light fill you, making you stronger and more aware.

Repeat this process for the papers numbered two through four.

When the burning of the last paper is complete, feel yourself transformed into a body of darkness like the night sky, and your blood transformed into light like the silver glow of the moon. Abide in this awareness knowing you are a child of Lilith, beyond duality.

Leave the candle burning on your altar or in your room until it has burned down. Take the ashes in the cauldron and bury them somewhere you feel drawn to. You do not forget the experiences of your past, but they no longer define you. Know that like your mother Lilith, you can do anything because you have overcome difficulty and pain, leaving the illusion of separation behind, and joining with her in unity.

Card: Wheel of Fortune
Letter: *Kaph* ךכ (Double letter)
Gematria: 20; but 500 when used as a final letter
Key: 10
Path: Mercy (*Hesed*) to Victory (*Netzach*)
Qlipothic Path: The Smiters (*Gha'ag Sheblah*) to The Ravens of Dispersion (*A'arab Zaraq*)

The Letter: *Kaph*

Kaph is the palm of the hand in the act of grasping. It is filled with sincerity (*Kavannah*). *Kaph* is a cup (*Kos*) filled with blessings. It is to honor thy mother and father (*Kibbud Ahv Va-Aim*). It is All (*Kol*). The first *sephirah, Keter,* starts with the letter *Kaph.* Only one who has been beaten (*Kattet*) and become pure (*Kasher*) shall drink of the cup. Wealth and poverty are the pair of opposites attributed to the double letter *Kaph*. These are the extremes of circumstances.

To grasp is to hold, to master, to comprehend. These ideas are in sharp contrast to the letter *Yod*. and the Hermit. "Rewarding Intelligence of Those Who Seek" is the Kabbalistic name of this mode of consciousness. *Kaph* concerns the establishment of harmony and order. It brings the fruition of "Seek and ye shall find." Reconciling apparent differences, *Kaph* leads to winning over seemingly antagonistic forces.

The *Qlipothic* Path: *Kaph*

In the *Qlipoth, Kaph* is the palm of the open hand of the dark manifestation that brings victory and conquest. Evolution is forced by opening new paths and possibilities leading beyond what was previously dictated. Luck is no longer in power, and change is certain.

The Tarot Card: The Wheel of Fortune (Key 10)

The Wheel of Fortune combines the ideas of rotation, cycles, whirling motion. and simultaneous ascent and descent (evolution and involution). Occult teaching asserts what appears to be by chance is not truly random. Every effect is the consequence of preceding causes.

At the corners of the card are the four animals mentioned in Ezekiel 1:10 and Revelation 4:7. They correspond to the fixed signs of the zodiac: The bull to Taurus; the lion to Leo; the eagle to Scorpio; the man to Aquarius. The numbers of these signs are 2, 5, 8, and 11, which add up to 26, the number of *Yahweh*. In this example the Y is the Lion, the first H is the Eagle, the V is the Man, and the final H is the Bull. Thus the "Living Creatures" signify the fixed, eternal modes of supernal consciousness. They are static compared to the turning wheel. That which was, is, and shall be remains ever the same, while everything rotates within it.

The wheel is the whole cycle of the cosmos. The circles within the wheel reflect the four lower *Olamot*, or universes. The eight spokes are the eight-pointed star in Key 17 and together represent the Universal Energy. A wavy serpent (suggesting light vibration) descends on the left side of the wheel, symbolizing the descent of the cosmic energy into the finite of name and form. Anubis (the Egyptian Jackal-headed God of the Dead) rises on the right side of the wheel to illustrate the evolution of consciousness from lower to higher forms.

The head of Anubis represents intellect, while his red color typifies desire and activity. The Sphinx at the top represents the true self, behind personality. When enlightenment comes, we become aware of what transcends personality. Inside the circle are the letters TARO and *YAHWEH*. TARO represents the number 671, which represents the *Sephirot Malkut*, or Kingdom.

Meditation With the Wheel of Fortune

Picturing yourself as the Tarot card is an immensely powerful meditative technique which can help you get in touch with the consciousness of the path.

- After performing primordial meditation, imagine yourself weightless, and picture yourself floating in a blue sky full of clouds.
- There is a giant wheel before you that represents all cycles, including those of the human soul.
- It is turning around and around.
- Near the wheel are a snake made of light on the left, a red Anubis on the right, and a blue sphynx on top.
- You realize this wheel is the wheel of incarnation and evolution which services all people.
- As you gaze at the wheel, you realize the snake of light is your soul first entering incarnation.
- The Anubis evokes the process of your evolution through many incarnations. You see these lives flash before your eyes.
- The Sphynx is your true, enlightened self. You see the potential of your perfection.
- Watch the wheel turn. What scenes does it reveal to you?
- Abide in this presence as long as you can.
- When finished, bring yourself back to normal awareness and exit the meditation.

Lilith Consciousness

Lilith's consciousness at this path is Ardat Lili *(also called* Lilitu*)*. She is a very ancient form of Lilith characterized by wings and associated with the air. In the ancient world, Ardat Lili was sometimes called upon to help treat mental illness. As stated, she was associated with the air, but also with crops and the cyclic nature of nurture and destruction. This consciousness nurtures what is helpful and destroys what is no longer of service.

Lilith Meditation

Turning the wheel is a moving meditation where you walk a circle and contemplate cycles by linking to Lilith's spirit. For this meditation you will need a candle on a stand, placed in the middle of a room.

- Light your candle, turn off the lights, and stand to the East of your candle, facing South.
- Perform the Kabbalistic Cross:
- Begin to slowly walk clockwise around the circle. Chant,
    - Ardat Lili, Ardat Lili, Ardat Lili.

- Contemplate the following cycles:
    - Day and Night
    - The Seasons
    - Life and Death
    - Reincarnation

- Any other cycles you can think of

When finished, stop walking the circle and blow out the candle.

Card: Justice
Letter: *Lamed* ל (Single letter)
Gematria: 30
Key: 11
Path: Severity (*Gevurah*) to Beauty (*Tiferet*)
Qlipothic Path: The Flaming Ones (*Golachab*) to The Disputers (*Thagirion*)

The Letter: *Lamed*

Lamed is tall and elegant like a palm branch (*Lulav*). *Lamed* is in night (*Lilah*), by the moon (*L'vanah*), and forever (*L'olam*). The body of the *Lamed* is curved by its heart (*Laev*) and soars like a flame (*Lahav*). This cosmic power is all-pervading and all-embracing, so there is no other power outside it. We must understand *Lamed* stands for something within the Life-power. It represents an inward urge and inward capacity for self- direction.

In the Hebrew Book of Formation (*Sefer Bahir*), the special function assigned to *Lamed* is "Work or Action". This is also the basic meaning of the Sanskrit word Karma.

The *Qlipothic* Path: *Lamed*

In the *Qlipoth, Lamed* is ox goad removed and broken so no force pushes the soul forward in domestication. Instead, it returns to its unbridled nature, tipping the scales of justice. This *Lamed* shows cosmic laws to be false and malleable so that anything is possible.

The Tarot Card: Justice (Key 11)

Our subconscious realizations from experience are the basis of all our activity. From them we gain instruction and knowledge. Faithful Intelligence is the mode of consciousness attributed to the letter Lamed. The Hebrew for faithful is AMN (Amen). This word is related to the Sanskrit *AUM* or *OM*.

Justice signifies the active administration of Law. It also makes us think of balance, poise, accuracy, equity, etc. The central figure is a personification of Justice, but she wears no blindfold. Her yellow hair is like the Empress' hair, and she can be associated with the woman who tames the lion in

Key 8 (Strength). Keys 8 and 11 represent different aspects of the same power. Her red and green robes represent action and imagination.

The gold scales are a reminder that outcome can be a measure of action. The sword is steel and is an indication all action destroys as well as builds. The general meaning of the Justice card is that gaining knowledge and experience helps us find balance, but balance also requires the elimination of useless, outworn forms. Our education is completed by action and work, because merely hearing something is not true education-action is required.

Meditation With Justice

Picturing yourself as the Tarot card is an immensely powerful meditative technique which can help you get in touch with the consciousness of the path.

- After performing primordial meditation, picture yourself as the figure in the Justice card.
- You are clothed in rich red robes with a green collar and there is a crown on your head.
- You hold an upraised sword in your right hand and a scale in your left.
- You sit on a throne between two pillars, with a purple cloth behind you and a yellow sky of divine light.
- Feel the sword and scale as they hold balance and bring justice to the universe. You are the cosmic and internal force of balance.

- Abide as this presence as long as you can.
- When finished, bring yourself back to normal awareness and exit the meditation.

Lilith Consciousness

At this path, Lilith consciousness is about breaking out of old patterns and replacing them with new ones that are closer to the soul's true nature. As humans we are literally programmed by culture and society to act in certain ways and to react accordingly. Some of these actions are beneficial, but some hurt us because they are contrary to our true nature. Lilith is a wild spirit who wants us to be our true selves. This does not mean free to hurt and abuse for our own amusement, but it also means not acting by societal expectations that smother important aspects of our true selves.

Lilith Meditation

The Silent Witness with Lilith is a meditation we explored earlier in this book. This time we are going to practice it with action. With this practice you will need a pen and paper.

- Get into a comfortable position.
- Push all thoughts aside and begin to breathe in a regular rhythm.
- Breathe in… and out… in… and out
- As thoughts arise, gently push them aside and refocus on your breathing.

- Call on Lilith to empower you and to be the lens of your mind which witnesses' events.
- Let your mind wander to the events of the day.
- Recall anything that went well or poorly. Set aside your judgement and let Lilith look at these events.
- As you breathe in, feel her analyzing what has transpired.
- As you breathe out, fee her speaking of what needs transformed. This is not judgement, but refinement.
- Abide in this state, repeating the process, until there are no more events to review.
- When this is complete you can return to normal consciousness and close the meditation.

After performing Silent Witness and finding an emotion, action, or other reaction which Lilith pointed out as not the best outcome for a situation, write it down. Make sure you read over the outcomes she wishes changed every day and explore ways that you could mitigate the reaction you had or how you handled the event. Next time one of these events occur, remember what you learned from Silent Witness and employ a different method of solving the issue.

Card: The Hanged Man
Letter: *Mem* מ ם (Mother letter – water)
Gematria: 40; but 600 when used as a final letter
Key: 12
Path: Severity (*Gevurah*) to Splendor (*Hod*)
Qlipothic Path: The Flaming Ones (*Golachab*) to The Poison of God (Samael)

The Letter: ***Mem***

Mem is the substance of Mother Earth and the stuff (*Mamash*) by which life in the world is sustained. It is water (*Mayim*), wilderness (*Midbar*) through which people wander and they are made ready. It is the food (*Ma-Achal*) and work (*M'La-Cha*) which is done for food. And it is the rest (*Minucha*) of the Shabbat. There are the Holy Commandments (*Mitzvot*), and the throne chariot of God (*Merkabah*). This is the second of three Mother letters in the Hebrew Alphabet. Its name literally means "seas," but like many plurals in Hebrew it designates a general idea, in this case, "water."

Alchemists call water the mother, seed, and root of all minerals. Water, represented by Mem, is the first mirror. Water reflects images upside down, and this idea is carried out by the symbolism of Key 12. This is life in a reflected image.

The *Qlipothic* Path: *Mem*

In the *Qlipoth Mem* is the water of the abyss. All restrictions of flow are dissolved so everything can drown in its dark depths. The cosmic flow of energy into form is reversed creating formlessness. The spirit is freed and allowed to manifest however it needs to for transformation.

The Tarot Card: The Hanged Man (Key 12)

The occult meaning of the Hanged man is "suspended mind." This card also reflects the dependence of the human personality on the super-conscious. The youth hangs from a T-cross made of living wood. The T-cross also stands for the Hebrew letter *Tav* (the last letter of the Hebrew Alphabet). His legs form a cross (for the number 4) and the lines from his arms to his hair form a reversed triangle (which is 3 because of 3 sides). Multiplying this together results in twelve—twelve zodiac signs and the complete cycle of manifestation.

The three represents the Empress who is the great womb. The four represents the Emperor. The hanged man's upper garment is blue (to symbolize water, the High Priestess, and universal mind) and his leggings are red (to symbolize the Emperor and the Hierophant). The man's head is surrounded by light, which symbolizes enlightenment. His pale hair suggests the Emperor and the Hermit. He is the ancient of days manifested in human form.

The man is turned upside down in a position contrary to that of most people. This signifies that the spiritual life is upside down from the normal way of living, speaking, thinking, and acting. Hence Jacob Boehme said the great secret is "to walk in all things contrary to the world."

Meditation With the Hanged Man

Picturing yourself as the Tarot card is an immensely powerful meditative technique which can help you get in touch with the consciousness of the path.

- After performing primordial meditation, picture yourself hanging upside down from a T cross.
- The bindings suspend you without discomfort, but you see everything from an inverted perspective.
- You are clothed in a blue tunic and red leggings.

- You feel warmth around your head as light shines all around it.
- Hang there in peace, seeing everything upside down and contemplate what it would be like to see everything in normal life from a different perspective.
- Abide as this presence as long as you can.
- When finished, bring yourself back to normal awareness and exit the meditation.

Lilith Consciousness

The consciousness of Lilith at this path is that of the *Lilin* and *Lilu,* Lilith's children. The tradition of *Quimbonda* has *Pomba Gira* (female) and *Exu* (male) spirits who are the children of Na'amah under Lilith as their goddess. The *Lilin* and *Lilu* are many, composed of the spirits of the dead and eternal spirits. In either case, they are freed from their pre-existing beliefs and constraints, becoming new beings in the freedom of Lilith.

Lilith Meditation

The point of the upside-down practice is to get consciousness to see things in a new way. For this meditation you will need a crystal ball. If one is not available, you can lie down and look up.

- Perform primordial meditation, focusing on your breath, pushing all thoughts aside.

- Chant the name Pomba Gira, Pomba Gira, Pomba Gira. Ask the spirit of the Lilin and Lilu to help you see in the ways that they see.
- Open your eyes and gaze into the crystal ball. You will notice that everything in the ball is upside down. If you are laying down and gazing upward, try to alter your focus to look at the room as if the ceiling is the floor and the floor is the ceiling.
- Imagine yourself in that upside-down place, navigating a world that is completely reversed from what you are normally used to.
- Contemplate what it would be like if the world suddenly shifted, and everything was contrary to how it is now.
- What if the world is contrary to how you perceive it? What if everything is somewhat different than humanity imagines? Contemplate the possibilities.

When you have explored enough, end the meditation, and return to normal consciousness.

Card: Death
Letter: *Nun* ן נ (Single letter)
Gematria: 50; but 700 when used as a final letter
Key: 13
Path: Beauty (*Tifferet*) to Victory (*Netzach*)
Qlipothic Path: The Disputers (*Thagirion*) to The Ravens of Dispersion (*A'arab Zaraq*)

The Letter: ***Nun***

Nun is the soul (*Neshamah*) and the personality display (*Nefesh*). She is feminine (*N'Kayva*) because she receives. There is something of melody (*Niggun*) which creates wonder (*Nifla-Ot*) within *Nun*. *Nun* is also faithful (*Neh-Emanah*), eternal light (*Ner Tamid*), and a spark (*Nitzotz*). *Nun* is pronounced like "noon" and as a noun means "fish." As a verb (since fish are prolific) it means "to sprout" or "to grow." The essential idea is fertility which is bound up in thought and language.

Motion is the function attributed to *Nun*. Change is the basis of manifestation and thus imaginative Intelligence is the mode of consciousness attributed to *Nun*. Kabbalists say, "It is the ground of similarity in the likeness of beings." this is the basis of similarity which is passed through procreation. All changes are really changes in mental imagery. Change the image and ultimately the outer form will change to reflect it.

The *Qlipothic* Path: *Nun*

In the *Qlipoth Nun* is the fish flowing through the waters of death. This fish is like salmon swimming against the current with no intentions of returning to their original home. *Nun* represents Q*Ayin* (Cain) who took life but was marked to never die. Q*Ayin* exists in an eternal state of unlife, flowing between both worlds.

The Tarot Card: Death (Key 13)

Key 13 is called Death. Judeo-Christian Scripture says death is the last enemy to be overcome. They also say, "Overcome evil with good. Love your enemies." These two brief sentences are the whole secret. The forces of change which result in physical death are bad only because we misunderstand and fear them. They are forces connected with reproduction, and by right use of imagination they may be tamed and transformed. Death, like every other event in human life, is a manifestation of the cycle of creation. When we understand the cycles, we can direct the forces of change and overcome death through consciousness. Yet understanding will never be ours until fear of death and dying is overcome by knowledge and by interpretation of the phenomena of physical dissolution.

The image on the card is a skeletal personification of death, riding a white horse. There are heads and hands in the earth below. Behind the rider is a river and the rising sun. The skeleton is the basis for all movement in the human body and is the framework which supports us. It is through death that society changes for the better come to pass. Old ideas pass away with the death of persons who hold them. New ideas gain potency as one generation comes to maturity. Thus, the fact of death is an instrument of progress.

Psychologically, the emphasis falls on imagination. Change your ideas and your old conception of personality dies. Change your intellectual patterns, and new ideas and perspective will be born. If your pattern is built with the ideas developed through self-surrender (as pictured by the hanged man), it will lead to a complete transformation of your personality. Little by little, there comes a complete readjustment of one's personal conceptions of life and its values. The change from the personal to the universal viewpoint is so radical that mystics often compare it to death.

Meditation With Death

Picturing yourself as the Tarot card is an immensely powerful meditative technique that can help you get in touch with the consciousness of the path.

- After performing primordial meditation, picture yourself as Death – a skeletal being in black armor, riding a white horse
- You are clothed in armor and holding a banner.
- It is early morning, and the sun is just rising.
- You can hear the water of the river rushing past the banks.
- When you look down, there are body parts around you.
- A pope-like figure in gold approaches you. He tries to convince you not to take life, but you have no choice, it is your duty.
- Abide as this presence as long as you can.
- When finished, bring yourself back to normal awareness and exit the meditation.

Lilith Consciousness

Lilith's consciousness in all her aspects is about transformation. At this path, her consciousness is especially focused on transformation through death and rebirth. In the *midrash*, *QAyin* (Cain), the first child of Adam and Eve is the spiritual child of Lilith and Samael. He kills his brother and then is marked to walk the earth for eternity. He exists in a state of living death where he never dies but doesn't truly live either. As painful as death is for those who lose loved ones, it is a necessary part of our transformation so we can become more. If we are devoted to Lilith, she will be with us through every transformation.

Lilith Meditation

Transformation comes in many ways. Facing death is one key step on our path.

- Find a local graveyard where you feel comfortable walking alone.
- When you enter the graveyard, drop a few small coins as offerings to the spirits that guard the cemetery.
- Ask for entrance and thank them for their service to the living and the dead. Chant names of Lilith – Lilith, Lilit, Lilu for a few minutes and let her enter your spirit. Ask her for her vision and direction.
- Start at one end of the cemetery and walk through it.
- Look at some of the gravestones, notice names, dates, and other details. If any particular grave draws you, spend some time at that site meditating on the person who is buried there and what their life may have been like.
- When you are comfortable, find a spot in the cemetery to stand or sit. Meditate on the fact you are there alive, and whole. Begin to accept that eventually your body may be one of those in the cemetery, but

your soul will continue. Even though the body you currently inhabit will be gone, your soul will not die.

- If you believe in reincarnation, picture that this has happened to you many times and will happen many more. You will inhabit a body, it will die and be disposed of, but you will continue.
- Know that Lilith is with you all along the way and you are not alone.

When you are ready, let go of the images and leave the cemetery.

Card: Temperance
Letter: *Samekh* ס (Single letter)
Gematria: 60
Key: 14
Path: Beauty (*Tifferet*) to Foundation (*Yesod*)
Qlipothic Path: The Disputers (*Thagirion*) to The Obscene Ones (*Gamaliel*)

The Letter: *Samekh*

Samekh dwells in a poor harvest hut (*Sukka*). It is also the mountain called *Sinai*. *Samekh* is also the shelter of the Holy One: prayers (*Siddur*), meals (*Seder*), books (*Sefer*), and the *Torah* (*Sefer Torah*). These lead one to a deeper secret (*Sod*). *Samekh* means tent peg or prop. It is what makes a tent secure and corresponds to what would now be suggested to us by the foundation of a house. *Samekh* be seen as the symbol for the foundation of the house of life.

Samekh is what sustains, preserves, and maintains our personal existence. The literal meaning of *Samekh* in Hebrew is "vibration." Vibration is the fundamental nature of the power which makes sight possible and is the source of all our strength. Vibration is the nature of manifestation. Tentative intelligence or intelligence of probation is the mode of consciousness associated with *Samekh*, where theory is put to the test of practical application. It therefore suggests adaption, equalization, or balance.

The *Qlipothic* Path: *Samekh*

In the *Qlipoth*, *Samekh* is the prop which holds up the Tree of Shadows, keeping it in place until full manifestation and transformation can be obtained. This force aids in the freeing of souls from the cycle of rebirth by tearing down the tent peg that holds the house together, while enabling new structures to be supported.

The Tarot Card: Temperance (Key 14)

At the bottom of the picture of the card is a pool, representing *Yesod* (the 9th *Sephirah* of the Tree of Life). This is the seat of the ego grasping of mankind. The path corresponding to Key 14 is Beauty (*Tiferet*) to the Crown (*Keter*). The end of this path of attainment is the realization of the crown of perfect union with the super-consciousness.

The angel of the Key is Michael—Archangel of Fire. His white robe represents purity and wisdom. At his neck are the letters *YHWH* (the Tetragrammaton). Below this is a triangle representing skill. One foot of the angel is in the water (symbol of cosmic consciousness) and the other is on land (symbol of concrete physical manifestation). There is a crown on the horizon, almost like a rising sun, representing the dawning of enlightenment. He is pouring water back and forth between two cups showing balance and the movement of thought between the cosmic super-conscious and physical manifestation.

The angel is the true "I Am" of the human race, our true self. He is shown adapting and modifying the personal stream of thought in the actions and reactions of the human personality. The implication of this is that we do nothing of ourselves in ego.

Meditation With Temperance

Picturing yourself as the Tarot card is an immensely powerful meditative technique that can help you get in touch with the consciousness of the path.

- After performing primordial meditation, picture yourself as the archangel Michael.

- You are clothed in a white robe with your red wings open behind you.
- Your right foot is on the land and your left foot is on the surface of the water, but you are completely balanced.
- There is a crown rising like the sun in the background.
- In each hand you have a cup, and you are transferring water back and forth.
- No matter how you move the cups, you never spill a drop. The water continually flows from one to the other.
- Understand that this is symbolic of consciousness being moved between realms.
- Abide as this presence as long as you can.
- When finished, bring yourself back to normal awareness and exit the meditation.

Lilith Consciousness

Lilith's consciousness at this path is as Lilith the Younger. Lilith the Younger is described as the daughter of a fallen angel and a human mother. She is the consort of Ashmedai (Asmodeus). Lilith the Younger's consciousness is closer to Na'amah than to Lilith, who is beyond physical creation. Lilith the Younger is a being of admixture who still has ties to her ego. This consciousness sifts energy from above and energy from below to make choices in the moment. Unlike Lilith the Elder who plays the long game, Lilith the Younger focuses on each moment to enable transformation.

Lilith Meditation

Previously in the section on Spheres, we worked with the physical practice called a *Mudra*. In this section we will use the *Mudra* to symbolize moving Lilith's energy down and through creation.

- Place your hands above your head in a reversed "V" where your elbows are bent, and your hands overlap.
- Say the name Lilith.
- Keep your hands in the same position but lower them down so that your arms are pointing.
- Say the name Lilit.
- This represents the arrow pointing up, then coming down, bringing energy and consciousness with it.
- Say the name Na'amah.
- Perform this moving meditation several times and focus on the idea of "As Above, So Below" – Lilith above and below.

Card: The Devil
Letter: *Ayin* ע (Single letter)
Gematria: 70
Key: 15
Path: Beauty (*Tifferet*) to Splendor (*Hod*)
Qlipothic Path: The Disputers (*Thagirion*) to The Poison of God (Samael)

The Letter: ***Ayin***

Ayin does not speak, it only sees because it is an eye. It is the silent humility (*Anavah*) of serving God, worshipping (*Avodah*) Him/Her. But some serve a God which is not living, like the golden calf (*Agel*) or another idol (*Avodah Zara*). This is the *Ayin* of slavery which shames (*Avadim Ha-Yinu*).

However, *Ayin* begins the Ten Commandments (*Aseret Ha-Dibrote*).

Ayin means eye or foundation and signifies the external, superficial appearance of things. Since the eye is the major way we experience the world around us, it represents all sensation. Our sight is limited to the field of vision, and we only see appearances. Hence the eye represents the limitations of the visible, and the bondage of ignorance resulting from accepting the limitations that appearances are all there is.

Laughter can purify the subconscious and dissolves mental complexes and conflicts. Renewing Intelligence is the mode of consciousness attributed to *Ayin*. This is directly related to mirth, because the perception of incongruities (that which does not fit) is what brings forth new ideas. When we find a fact which does not fit in with our beliefs, we are obliged to revise our theories, unless we are the sort who prefers a comfortable lie to an uncomfortable truth.

The *Qlipothic* Path: *Ayin*

In the *Qlipoth, Ayin* is the all-seeing eye of the dragon of the void. This eye of no-thingness can see beyond all illusion and outer appearances. It reveals the inner truth and reality inside and behind all things. They eye of *Ayin* reveals the perverse nature of that which restricts and limits without reason, freeing the soul to let go of ego.

The Tarot Card: The Devil (Key 15)

The symbolism of Key 15 represents the cruder forms of man's answers to the question, "What keeps me from expressing who I really am?" At the same time, this picture indicates the correct solution to the problem, and points to the way which leads out of difficulty.

The Devil is the English for the Hebrew Satan, adversary. The picture refers to man's ideas concerning the nature of what seems to oppose his struggles for freedom. Remember, the Devil personifies the serpent-power in the letter *Tet* and by Key 8, Strength. The name for the serpent which tempted Eve is *Nakash,* and the gematria of this word is 358, the value of Messiah.

The digits 15 (from Key 15) reduce to 6 (1+5), the number of the Lovers and so this card is a foil for the Lovers card. Furthermore 15 is the sum of numbers from 0 to 5, so the Hierophant (5) is also related. Compare The Devil to The Lovers and The Hierophant. The background of the card is black, color of darkness, ignorance, and limitation, implying that these qualities are the underlying cause of bondage.

The ridiculous figure of the Devil is a veil for a profound secret of practical occultism. The Devil is the opposite of the angel in the preceding card. He is also the caricature of the angel over the heads of the lovers, as the figures below the devil are bestial representations of the man and woman in Key 6.

The goat's horns on the Devil's head represents Capricorn. His bat wings symbolize the powers of darkness. He has the ears of a donkey, evoking the obstinacy and stubbornness of materialism. His body is half masculine and half feminine because both sexes can suffer from those qualities. Between his horns is a white, inverted pentagram. This is a key to the whole meaning of the figure.

The pentagram is a symbol of humanity. Inverted, it signals a reversal of man's place in the cosmos. In fact, the mistaken estimate of man's powers and possibilities is what keeps any one person in bondage. The Devil's uplifted right hand has all its fingers open—in contradiction to the Hierophant. This states that what my senses shows me is all there is.

On the palm of this open hand is the symbol for Saturn, which stands for limitation, inertia, and therefore ignorance. In the Devil's left hand is a torch, a phallic symbol, representing the transmission of life from generation to generation. Because this Devil has a navel, he is the product of humanity, produced from mankind's ignorance. His feet are the claws of an eagle. This corresponds to the sign Scorpio (which was originally symbolized by an eagle) and refers to the misuse of sexual power.

The Devil sits on a half cube, which means he only has half knowledge of the fabric of creation, the visible, sensory side of existence. The figures chained to the half cube represent self-conscious and sub-conscious modes of human mentality. Their horns, hoofs, and tails show that when reasoning is based only on surface appearances, human consciousness becomes bestialized. Notice that although they are chained to the cube, the loops are so large they might lift them off their heads. Their bondage is imaginary.

The Devil is sensation, divorced by ignorance from understanding. Yet he is also what brings renewal because we can make no real effort to be free until we feel our limitations.

Meditation With the Devil

Picturing yourself as the Tarot card is an immensely powerful meditative technique which can help you get in touch with the consciousness of the path.

- After performing primordial meditation, picture yourself as the man in the Devil card.
- It is dark and full of shadows.
- You know the devil or adversary is behind you, but you feel powerless.
- You are naked and there is a chain wrapped around your neck holding you to the Devil. You are caught in self-doubt and deprecation.
- You look over at the woman, who is also chained to the devil. You realize she is your sub-conscious. She is also caught in negative thought patterns.
- Remember who you really are, and flash back to the scene of the Lovers. Look at the woman and study her.

- After a time, she also remembers the Lovers, and she looks up at the devil. As soon as she truly sees him, his spell is broken.
- The darkness turns to light, the devil becomes an angel, and both you and the woman easily slip the chains off, they dissolve.
- Abide as this presence, the newly-free man, as long as you can.
- When finished, bring yourself back to normal awareness and exit the meditation.

Lilith Consciousness

At this path, Lilith's consciousness is focused on being able to see with true sight. She discerns what is transformative and what is hindering. She sees with the perspective of eternity and not temporary gain. Our eyes can deceive us because we make assumptions about what we see that may be wrong and are not in the big picture of our myriad lives; however Lilith sees with the view of everything for all time.

Lilith Meditation

If you have a need to break ties with a person, your past, or a negative habit, use this simple ritual. For this practice, you will need a candle, incense and an athame (knife).

- Light a candle and burn incense.

- Take up your athame (severity) with your left hand (severity).
- Call upon Lilith and ask her to be the movement of severity – restriction in your actions. Ask her to help you break ties and reset everything to a relationship with her.
- Make cutting motions in the air, first from right to left and then left to right. You will be making an X in the air in front of you with the knife.
- State the following invocation:
    - I cut all ties with [fill in what is to be cut away]
    - I am not owned by [fill in what is to be cut away]
    - I belong to only myself and Lilith.
    - Any bindings that hold me are broken.
    - Any bonds that constrict me are gone.
    - As it is spoken, so it is done.

Leave the candle burning on your altar until it burns out.

Card: The Tower
Letter: *Peh* ףפ (Double letter)
Gematria: 80; but 800 when used as a final letter
Key: 16
Path: Victory (*Netzach*) to Splendor (*Hod*)
Qlipothic Path: The Ravens of Dispersion (*A'arab Zaraq*) to The Poison of God (Samael)

The Letter: *Peh*

Peh is a mouth with no eyes and because it has no eyes everything seems simple (*P'Sha*t). Open the gates *(Pit-Chu Sh'Arim*) because everything is a miracle (*Peleh*). Know there is an orchard (*Pardes*) whose corners (*Payot*) belong to the poor and its fruit (*P'Ree*) is the hidden wisdom. *Peh* means the mouth as an organ of speech.

Because *Peh* is a mouth, it therefore symbolizes the power of utterance, and out of it come the issues of life. Beauty and Ugliness are the pair of opposites attributed to the letter *Peh* because human speech result in one or the other. Sin (or missing the mark) results in maladjustment or ugliness. Hitting the mark (being one's true self) results in the manifestations of beauty.

Active or exciting intelligence is the mode of consciousness attributed to *Peh*. It stirs up activity, sets things in motion, produces changes, and effects transformations.

The *Qlipothic* Path: *Peh*

In the *Qlipoth*, *Peh* is the mouth of the dragon of the void. This is the mouth of *Leviathan* and *Behemoth*, consuming all which is not needed so that it may be transformed and refined. This energy brings the black sun into full light within the realm of death, aiding in the ascent instead of descent of spirit.

The Tarot Card: The Tower (Key 16)

The Tower refers traditionally to the Tower of Babel where human languages were dispersed from a single, universal one. The lightning flash is the power drawn from above by the Magician. It is the sword of the Charioteer, the scepter of the Emperor, the force which turns the Wheel of Fortune, the scythe of Death, and the light from the Hermit's lantern. It breaks down existing forms to build new ones.

The lightning flash is also from Kabbalah—the path down the Tree of Life. In terms of consciousness, the lightning symbolizes a sudden, momentary flash of inspiration which breaks down ignorance. The falling figures recall the chained figures from The Devil card. They fall headfirst because the sudden influx of spiritual consciousness completely upsets the relationship between sub consciousness and self-consciousness.

The figures wear red and blue to show a mix of the sub-conscious and self-consciousness. One figure is crowned to show false knowledge, in which subconscious motives are permitted to dominate the personality. This domination of personality by emotion is overcome by spiritual awakening.

The crown falling from the Tower is the materialistic notion that matter is the ruling principles of existence. The tower is on a lonely peak and suggests the fallacy of personal isolation. There are 22 Hebrew *Yods* hanging in the air on either side of the building. They represent the Hebrew Alphabet and the 22 major arcana. Ten on one side are in the form of the Tree of Life. The other twelve show the zodiac. They hang in air to represent that their forces do not rest on any physical foundation. This picture corresponds to the second stage of spiritual enlightenment, in which a series of sudden inspirations lead to the understanding that the structures of false knowledge are not true. At this stage, the seeker suffers the destruction of his whole former philosophy.

Meditation With the Tower

Picturing yourself as the Tarot card is an immensely powerful meditative technique which can help you get in touch with the consciousness of the path.

- After performing primordial meditation, picture yourself standing on a valley, looking up at the Tower.
- Lightning strikes and destroys the Tower.
- Bricks and other man-made items come showering down off the cliff.
- A crown comes flying down and lands a few feet from you.
- What is left of the Tower, bursts into flame.
- Contemplate the destruction of old paradigms and falsehoods.
- When finished, bring yourself back to normal awareness and exit the meditation.

Lilith Consciousness

As stated previously, Kabbalists say the world is a play of beauty and horror. The horror of the world is destruction, violence, and death because of the emotions and loss humans feel from such events. Lilith's consciousness at this path is destruction and it is horror. Her transformation is not evil, and she will comfort her children through loss, but she also knows that destruction is necessary for transformation, so she brings the change in whatever way is necessary.

Lilith Meditation

Find an item that represents false ideas or ways of being that you no longer wish to associate with. For this practice, you will need a candle, incense, and a tool to destroy what you are letting go of (scissors, hammer, etc.).

- Light a candle and burn incense.
- Put the item which symbolizes what you want to break with in front of you. Picture it as whatever holds you back.
- Chant the name Lilit, Lilit, Lilit.
- Say, "Lilith, come and oversee the destruction of the husk around me."
- Take the tool you are going to use to destroy the item in your left hand (to symbolize severity).
- Cut or smash the item.
- State the following invocation:
    - I shatter the false ideas and ways of being from my past.
    - This item that I have destroyed cuts me off from these lies.
    - I belong to only myself and Lilith.
    - The falsehoods are shattered.
    - I am free to be who I truly am.
    - As it is spoken, so it is done.

Leave the candle burning on your altar until it burns out.

Card: The Star
Letter: *Tzaddi* ץצ (Single letter)
Gematria: 90; but 900 when used as a final letter
Key: 17
Path: Victory (*Netzach*) to Foundation (*Yesod*)
Qlipothic Path: The Ravens of Dispersion (*A'arab Zaraq*) to The Obscene Ones (*Gamaliel*)

The Letter: *Tzaddi*

Even though *Tzaddi* is not the first letter in the *Torah* or the *Aleph-bet,* it is the first letter God created, because *Tzaddi* is righteousness and giving is the very "foundation of the world" (*Tsedek*). It is the constriction (*Tzim-Tzum*). A righteous one is a *Tzaddik,* and a congregation a *Tsibur*

Ts'Daka. *Tzaddi* means "fishhook," signifying what draws the fish (*Nun*) out of the water (*Mem*).

The water is reflected personal existence, symbolized by the hanged man. The fish symbolizes transforming and reproductive power. *Tzaddi* is what lifts us up out of the material and uses our ability to create in order to bring about our enlightenment. A fishhook is a symbol for experimentation, quest, and research. It is a quest for what is not definitely realized yet.

Meditation is the function attributed to *Tzaddi*. It is the fishing for truth in the depths of the subconscious. The Hebrew word literally means "conception" and is the building of ideas. These are the early stages of enlightenment where the ego is still in control most of the time, thus meditation the safest practice because it draws nerve force up from the reproductive centers without fixation on the centers themselves. Natural intelligence is the mode of consciousness attributed to *Tzaddi*.

The *Qlipothic* Path: *Tzaddi*

In the *Qlipoth Tzaddi* is the fishhook used by the fisherman of the dark waters of the abyss. The fisherman hooks souls for the purpose of being saved from spiritual descent. The power of *Tzaddi* elevates the lower astral into higher realms bringing about formlessness. *Tzaddi* represents the power that can raise one up by its own means instead of depending on outside forces.

The Tarot Card: The Star (Key 17)

Because the number 17 can be reduced to 8 (1+7), there is a correspondence between this card and Strength (Key 8). It shows the method by which knowledge of the spiritual world is attained. This method solves the mysteries of nature and unveils her to the enlightened. The yellow star signifies the energy which emanates from all the suns of the universe. It has eight points, and like the Wheel of Fortune or the symbols on the dress of the Fool, it symbolizes solar energy.

The seven smaller stars correspond to the Chakras. The mountain in the background represents the work of enlightenment. The bird on the bush is a scarlet ibis, sacred to Hermes, the Magician. Its long bill is a natural fishhook. It is perched on a tree, which represents the human brain and nervous system, symbolizing the act of bringing thoughts to rest through concentration. We have to stop thinking in order to meditate properly, and when we stop thinking, truth unveils herself to us.

The woman on the card represents the Empress, the High Priestess, and the woman on the Strength card. The pool is universal consciousness, which is activated by mediation. This is depicted by the water flowing into the pool from the right-hand path. The stream flowing from the other pitcher divides into five paths, mirroring the five physical senses. The earth supports the woman's weight, but she balances herself by water, the third stage of enlightenment. The depiction of this card is the calm which follows the storm.

Meditation With the Star

Picturing yourself as the Tarot card is an immensely powerful meditative technique which can help you get in touch with the consciousness of the path.

- After performing primordial meditation, picture yourself as the woman in the The Star card.
- It is night, and you are kneeling at the side of a pool. Your left leg supports you on the land while your right leg is bent over the water.
- You have two jugs with water flowing out of them. The one on the left is pouring onto the ground, and the one on the right is pouring into the pond.
- There is a huge 8-pointed star in the sky and 7 smaller ones surrounding it. The light is bright, and it almost looks like daytime.
- What you notice is that the water you are pouring never runs out. The water is eternal consciousness which flows through you and into the pull of the super conscious and onto the physical world, connecting them all.
- Abide in this awareness as long as you can.
- When finished, bring yourself back to normal awareness and exit the meditation.

Lilith Consciousness

At this path, Lilith's consciousness is about using everything to break free from the force of reincarnation. Reincarnating is not negative; it serves a purpose. However, for most the pull back into the cycle of birth, death, and rebirth is unconscious, and the soul has no choice in its next incarnation. Lilith always wants to bring choice so that her children transform with consent and knowledge of their path. When we link to Lilith, we can choose how we move through the world and the afterlife.

Lilith Meditation

Meditation is the best way to find the stillness needed to access our true self. Gratitude is another way to help break the fear and isolation of false ideas. The purpose of this practice is to meditate on things you are grateful for. For this practice, you will need a candle, incense, and a list of things you are grateful for.

- Light a candle and burn incense.
- Perform primordial meditation.
- Call on Lilith as the Queen of Heaven and Mistress of the Abyss.
- She is the blessing of all things.
- After a time, chant in your head all the things you are grateful for.
- Keep this up as long as you can.
- When finished, bring yourself back to normal awareness and exit the meditation.

Leave the candle burning on your altar until it burns out.

Card: The Moon
Letter: *Qoph* ק (Single letter)
Gematria: 100
Key: 18
Path: Victory (*Netzach*) to Kingdom (*Malkut*)
Qlipothic Path: The Ravens of Dispersion (*A'arab Zaraq*) to The Queen of the Night (Lilith)

The Letter: *Qoph*

The bottom of the letter *Qoph* is a man calling "Holy." The top of the letter *Qoph* is the Holy one reaching down. Qoph is the voice of an angel calling, "holy holy holy" (*Kodesh Kodesh Kadesh*), and it is the Lord of Hosts (*Yahweh Tzavaot*). Qoph is the voice (*Kol*) of a person proclaiming the unity of God (*K'ri-at Shema*). With the upper mark of the *Qoph*, God whispers very softly with a voice which is still and small (*Kol D'mama Daka*).

Qoph represents the back of the head. This is the part of the skull which contains the cerebellum and the medulla oblongata. By some it is called the reptilian brain. Qoph represents what comes before true consciousness; states of consciousness that proceed perfect control. Sleep is the function assigned to *Qoph,* which is the period of physiological repair.

The *Qlipothic* Path: *Qoph*

In the *Qlipoth, Qoph* is the back of the head of the serpent. This represents the reptilian brain within all humans as our nocturnal and lunar impulse. This letter influences the soul through sleep by creating lucidity and intuition. Because this force breaks the obsessive aspect of the ego during slumber it can uplift the lower aspects of the personality and soul to greater heights.

The Tarot Card: The Moon (Key 18)

The processes in this card are the direct outcome of the wheels within wheels of the rotations of cosmic cycles. At the same time, there is a point in human evolution, represented by the Hanged Man, at which we are aware that personality is only an instrument of the universal forces active in the supernal consciousness. This card is also related to the sign of Pisces governing the feet which are the path makers.

This card symbolizes body consciousness. The key number 18 is 9 (1+8) by reduction, showing that the Hermit is the goal of the path shown in this picture. In The Hermit we are united, according to occult teaching, whenever we experience dreamless sleep. Profound sleep is the state in which personal consciousness is perfectly joined to the true self.

The Moon stands for the reflected light of subconsciousness. The drops of light are each the letter *Yod;* this refers to the descent of the life-force from above into the material world. The pool below is the same as shown in the 14th and 17th keys, and it is the "great deep" of cosmic consciousness out of which emerges physical manifestation. From it, all organic life originates.

The pool also refers to the 9th *sephirah, Yesod,* which is known as the sphere of the moon, and is man as the sub-conscious. The lobster climbing from the pool is a symbol of the early stages of conscious unfoldment. The path, raising and falling, has been worn by those who have traveled this way before. It passes between a wolf and a dog because our path is one between our natural conditions and our enlightenment.

The path also symbolizes general knowledge, until it comes to the two towers, which mark the boundaries of the unknown and beyond. The path rises and falls, suggesting vibration. Yet it continually ascends, so as one progresses, the time comes when his most depressed states of consciousness are at a higher level than some of his earlier ones. Key 18 represents the 4th stage of spiritual enlightenment, where the knowledge gained by meditation is incorporated into the physical body.

Meditation With the Moon

Picturing yourself as the Tarot card is an immensely powerful meditative technique which can help you get in touch with the consciousness of the path.

- After performing primordial meditation, picture yourself as the moon. You are high in the dark night sky, radiating on the world.
- Below you are a pond and a path. Coming out of the water is a lobster.
- On one side of the path is a dog and on the other is a wolf. They look down the path which passes between towers and goes to an unknown land.
- Light in the form of the letter *Yod* rains down from you onto the land.
- You realize your light is the energy of change, evolution, and progress. Sometimes this light can manifest what looks like insanity, as beings are transformed and they pass through boundaries in their consciousness.
- Abide in this awareness as long as you can.

- When finished, bring yourself back to normal awareness and exit the meditation.

Lilith Consciousness

At this path, Lilith's consciousness is marked by her wild side. Lilith is not a tame being who does what is expected of her. She does have compassion and wants what is best for her children, but sometimes her methods defy logic and are more about passion. Her desire is for all beings to embody their true selves, who they can be without staying programmed by attachment and aversion. This is not to say she wants complete chaos because she has many children at different stages of their development; however, she does want us to let go of anything holding us back from being our authentic selves.

Lilith Meditation

Sometimes we must let go and just be – in a seeming state of lunacy. This is difficult when we are with others or when we feel we need to have it all together. This practice is one to let go and let your wild side manifest.

- Find a warm night when the moon is visible in any of its forms. Know that the moon is Lilith watching over you and fueling your passions.
- Put-on loose-fitting clothes and go barefoot.
- Go outside under the moon and let yourself go.

- Dance, sing, crawl, roll around, do whatever you feel lead to do.
- When finished, go back inside, and remember what it was like to let go and be.

Card: The Sun
Letter: *Resh* ר (Double letter)
Gematria: 200
Key: 19
Path: Splendor (*Hod*) to Foundation (*Yesod*)
Qlipothic Path: The Ravens of Dispersion (*A'arab Zaraq*) to The Poison of God (Samael)

The Letter: ***Resh***

Resh symbolizes the inescapable wish to believe you are closer to the divine than everyone else (*Yetzer Ha- Ra*). *Resh* goes up and down in the land as a gossip (*Rachil*). But there is another kind of *Resh*; the end of pretending—*Rosh Hashana,* the day of admitting. Let the Master of the Universe (*Ribono Shel Olam*) have compassion (*Rachamim*) on His children. *Resh* means the head and face of man because in the head are gathered all the distinctively human powers. Similarly, the word "countenance" is derived from a Latin verb meaning "to hold together or contain."

The *Qlipothic* Path: *Resh*

In the *Qlipoth, Resh* is the face of the serpent. It breaks the focus of logic to bring forward intuition and inner knowledge. *Resh* breaks anything which represses creativity and the inner voice. This energy is counter to whatever stops this flow, and manifest from deep within the soul.

The Tarot Card: The Sun (Key 19)

The Sun is the heavenly body corresponding to *Resh*. It reaches its highest manifestation in reason, the ruling force which makes effective the law symbolized in Strength. Fruitfulness and sterility are the pair of opposites attributed to *Resh*. The sun causes all growth, but it also makes deserts.

Collective Intelligence is the mode of consciousness for this card. The tasks of Collective Intelligence are to assemble, to bring together, to combine, to unify, to embody, and to synthesize. The Collective Intelligence concentrates all states of consciousness which have gone before and embodies them together in a new form. Thus, it is a regenerative mode of consciousness, incorporating all the elements of control in a new realization of personality.

As the number 19 (Key number) can be reduced to 10 (1+9), and 10 to 1 (1+0), this card relates to the Magician and the Wheel of Fortune. It is the final form of a series of keys involving self-conscious intelligence. The name of the card refers to the sun with a human face. It represents the truth that material forces of nature are really modes of conscious energy. The rays of the sun alternate waves and straight lines. The wavy rays represent vibration, and the straight ones represent radiation.

Four sunflowers, representing the four Kabbalistic universes and the four kingdoms of nature (mineral, vegetable, animal, and human) turn toward the child. The wall in the background represents human adaptation of natural conditions, relating to human speech. The wall is stone and represents the Hebrew word *ABN*. This is the union between Father and Son (*Abba* and *Ben*). Human speech is the manifestation of this union of the super-conscious with the self-conscious. The wall has five courses, symbolizing the five human senses because words are limited to describing things we experience through the physical sense, even though speech cannot adequately represent spiritual experience and higher levels of consciousness.

The child is shown with his back to the wall, where he or she is travelling beyond speech and the five senses. The child is not yet an adolescent, showing this is not full enlightenment, but a stage along the way. The child rides a white horse, being a vehicle of the enlightenment process, something natural yet under human control. This union is a grade of conscious self-identification with the consciousness of *Ain Sof Or* (endless light). Yet it is not final. The physical forces are under the control of the adept– "A little child shall lead them." A person at this level still feels himself to be a separate and distinct entity. It is not full liberation, but a higher level than the ones before it.

Meditation With the Sun

Picturing yourself as the Tarot card is an immensely powerful meditative technique which can help you get in touch with the consciousness of the path.

- After performing primordial meditation, picture yourself as the Sun. You are high in the sky, radiating light on the world.
- Below you is a wall with sunflowers growing behind it. The sunflowers are pointed outward beyond the wall.
- There is a child, free and happy riding a horse.
- You realize your light is not just warm and bright but also the light of consciousness flowing to all living beings. The child is soaking up your light as he/she realizes they are a manifestation of the All.
- Abide in this awareness as long as you can.
- When finished, bring yourself back to normal awareness and exit the meditation.

Lilith Consciousness

At this level, Lilith's consciousness is the divine muse that inspires us to creativity and brings transformation for ourselves and others. True creativity comes from passion. Who better than a goddess considered a succubus to help us focus our passion into creative acts?

Lilith Meditation

As much as we need to let go and just be, sometimes we need to soak up energy. This can be useful for us to be reenergized and empowered.

- Pick a relatively warm and sunny day or moonlit night, depending on your preference.
- Find a comfortable spot (if during the day either in the shade or wear sunscreen to protect your skin).
- Get into a comfortable position.
- Call on Lilith as the power that fuels you. You can chant her name or just think of her. She is the sun or the moon, whichever is shining down on you.
- Push all thoughts aside and begin to breath in a regular rhythm.
    - Breath in… and out… in… and out
- As thoughts arise, gently push them aside and refocus on your breathing.
- Feel your soul drinking in the air and the sun or moon's energy (depending on if it is day or night).

- Let inspiration for creative acts fill you. When the meditation is over, take up your brush, your pen, or whatever you use to create, and do it in the name of Lilith.
- When finished, bring yourself back to normal awareness and exit the meditation.

Card: Judgement
Letter: *Shin* ש (Mother letter – fire)
Gematria: 300
Key: 20
Path: Splendor (*Hod*) to Kingdom (*Malkut*)
Qlipothic Path: The Poison of God (Samael) to The Queen of Night (Lilith)

The Letter: *Shin*

Something of *Shin* is shattering, like the shattering of the primeval vessels (*Sh'vi-Rat Ha-Kalim*). Sound the great ram's horn (*Shofar*). Bring back home all who have been banished; gather the broken pieces. *Shin* is the letter just before the end. It is the fitting together of all the parts. *Shin* is peace (*Shalom*); completion; wholeness. At the end is rest, which is the seventh day (*Shabbat*). *Shin* is also the beginning of God's most mysterious name, *Shaddai*. *Shin* means tooth, probably a serpent's fang. It suggests sharpness, acidity, and active manifestation.

The gematria of 300 is the same as *Ruach Elohim*, which means the holy life breath. This letter is a symbol of the power which tears down the limitations of form as teeth break up food. It represents the power which "kills" the false personality and its sense of separateness. Fire is the element attributed to Shin. It is also the quality of the Tarot cards the Emperor, Strength, and Temperance. Its color is scarlet.

The *Qlipothic* Path: *Shin*

In the *Qlipoth, Shin* is the fangs of the serpent, which injects fire into the spirit. This fiery manifestation is the most forceful of all the powers bringing destruction and emulation of anything standing in the way of change. *Shin* devours all forces of creation so that chaos and void can manifest, bringing no-thingness.

The Tarot Card: Judgment (Key 20)

Perpetual Intelligence is the mode of consciousness for this card. Its name is derived from a Hebrew root meaning "to stretch." Because this is an extension beyond the limits of consciousness common to most human beings, implying conscious immortality. The number 20 reduces to 2 (2+0), and we understand the consciousness here is the culmination of mental activities originating in the memory of the High Priestess. This key implies completion, decision, termination. It is the final state of personal consciousness. The figures in the picture are a man, a woman, and a child whose bodies are tinted grey, to represent that in this phase of personal consciousness opposites have been neutralized, as complementary colors are neutralized in grey. It also symbolizes that the scene depicted is not located in the physical plane.

The man is self-consciousness, the woman is sub-consciousness, and the child is regenerated personality. The position of their arms represents *LVX*, which means "light" in Latin. The angel Gabriel pictured in the card is divine breath. The action of heat upon water creates air, the substance of breath. Seven basic tones are indicated by seven lines radiating from the bell of the trumpet. These seven tones are those which affect the seven chakras by sympathetic vibration.

The coffins float upon a sea, which is the final reservoir of those waters beginning in the robe of the High Priestess. The coffins are rectangular, to represent the three dimensions of the physical plane. The three human figures are at right angles to the coffins to suggest the fourth dimension. The child's back is toward us because he implies return to source. This card shows the sixth stage of spiritual unfoldment, in that personal consciousness is on the verge of blending with the universal. At this stage there is realization personal existence is joining between self-consciousness and subconsciousness as they link to the super-conscious. This fourth- dimensional experience blots out the delusion of separateness forever.

Meditation With Judgement

Picturing yourself as the Tarot card is an immensely powerful meditative technique which can help you get in touch with the consciousness of the path.

- After performing primordial meditation, picture yourself as the man in the card Judgement.
- You can feel the wood of the coffin below you and the gentle rocking of water beneath.
- You are looking up at the angel Gabriel.
- Across from you is a woman who is your partner, and she is also looking up at the angel.
- Between you and the woman is a child who is connected to both of you and the child is looking up at the angel as well.
- You realize that your thoughts and emotions, your very consciousness is shared by you, the woman, the child, and the angel.
- You are all one. You are the conscious mind, the woman is the sub-conscious, the angel is the super-conscious, and the child is the integration of all.
- Shift your consciousness between the different figures and then settle into the child.
- Feel yourself as the integration of all as a completely unified being.

- Abide in this unity for as long as you can.
- When finished, bring yourself back to normal awareness and exit the meditation.

Lilith Consciousness

Lilith consciousness at this path is Na'amah. Na'amah is a physical incarnation of Lilith who was the sister of Tubal-Cane and the wife of Noah. After her death she returned to be a spiritual incarnation of Lilith at *Malkut* on the Tree of Life and Lilith on the Tree of Shadows. Her name means "pleasant," because she was quite beautiful. However, Na'amah is not a pushover. She can be quite strong and powerful, striving to get what she thinks is the best outcome. As the enlightened Norea, she even burnt down the arc after Noah first built it because he would not do as she asked, and he had to rebuild. Na'amah's will is a raging fire which brings transformation no matter what the cost.

Lilith Meditation

Life Review is based on the Silent Witness practice of merely observing mental-emotional states, and all the thoughts and feelings-emotions that arise, without any judgment or attachment and aversion.

When you are done, see how everything in your life has led to your current state and to your eventual enlightenment and liberation. This meditation is a longer practice, so make sure you have time allotted to accomplish it.

- Get into a comfortable position.
- Push all thoughts aside and begin to breath in a regular rhythm.
- Breathe in... and out... in... and out
- As thoughts arise, gently push them aside and refocus on your breathing.
- Call on Na'amah to empower you and to be the lens of your mind that witnesses events.
- Start on a tour of the major events of your life.
- Recall anything that went well or poorly. Set aside your judgment and let Na'amah look at these events.
- As you breathe in, feel her analyzing what has transpired.
- As you breathe out, feel her speaking of what needs transformed. This is not judgment, but refinement.
- Realize that some events which may not have seemed to go well, served a purpose to move your further on your path. Our journey is not a linear one.
- Abide in this state, repeating the process, until there are no more events to review.
- When this is complete, you can return to normal consciousness and close the meditation.
- After the meditation is over, take stock of your life and take pride in all you have accomplished. If anything does not serve your good, ask Na'amah to help you make adjustments to see change and transformation.

Card: The World
Letter: *Tav* ת (Double letter)
Gematria: 400
Key: 21
Path: Foundation (*Yesod*) to Kingdom (*Malkut*)
Qlipothic Path: The Obscene Ones (*Gamaliel*) to The Queen of Night (*Lilith*)

The Letter: ***Tav***

Tav is the mark that deity writes on man and is the letter both have in common. *Tav* is the sound of man singing God's praises: Psalms (*Tehilim*). And it is the sound of man returning to God (*Teshuva*). *Tav* is also the sound of God speaking to man through His/Her Scriptures (*Torah, Tanach,* and *Talmud*).

Tav proves that a letter can capture something of man and God. Therefore, *Tav* is also mending (*Tikkune*).

Tav means signature or mark and is a cross of equal arms, like that on the breast of the high priestess. This letter is *Tau* in the Greek Alphabet and the Egyptian Tau-cross is said to have been a tally for measuring the depth of the Nile. Among the Hebrews it was a symbol of salvation. Thus, it represents salvation from death and eternal life in full conscious awareness. The letter *Tav* indicates the final seal and witness to the completion of liberation. Center, or "the palace of holiness" is the direction attributed to *Tav*. This palace of holiness is said to "sustain all things."

The Hebrew word for palace is *Haikal*. Its gematria is 65, which is also the number of *Adonai* (Lord). Dominion and Slavery is the pair of opposites attributed to *Tav*. The understanding of the necessity for limitation in manifestation is the secret of dominion. Wrong understanding of the same thing is the cause of our slavery to conditions around us. The clue to the right understanding is "He who would rule nature must first obey her laws." Administrative Intelligence is the mode of consciousness attributed to *Tav* which is consciousness of active participation in cosmic processes. It is entry into the upper universes as a fully enfranchised citizen, charged with full responsibility for the execution of its laws. The number 21 (of the Key) relates to 12 and 3. It is also the sum of the numbers from 0 to 6.

The *Qlipothic* Path: *Tav*

In the *Qlipoth Tav* is the mark which sets those apart who are destined to walk the path of *Nod*. This separates a being from the cosmic order lifting the soul out of matter and into the abyss. As with this path on the Tree of Life, *Tav* in the Tree of Shadows represents a cross. In this case it is not a cross which represents matter, but one that creates a liminal space between worlds.

The Tarot Card: The World (Key 21)

The card is called The World, but sometimes it is called The Universe to indicate that the consciousness it represents is cosmic. The four animals at the corners of the design have been explained in connection with the tenth key of the tarot (the fixed signs of the zodiac to represent all types of humanity). The ellipse is formed of 22 groups of three leaves, eleven groups on either side. These represent the 22 forces corresponding to the letters of the Hebrew Alphabet and the keys of the Tarot. There are three leaves in each group, because each one of the 22 forces have three modes of expression (mercy, severity, or compassion).

The horizontal 8-shaped bindings at the top and bottom of the wreath are like those in The Magician and Strength as eternity. Here they are red because they have been carried into action. Their position symbolizes, "As above, so below." The dancer represents the merging of self-consciousness with subconsciousness and the binding of these two with super-consciousness. The violet scarf conceals the fact that the figure is androgynous. In this form of consciousness, all sense of separate sex is lost with the extinction of all sense of separate personality.

This is the all-father and all-mother. She is the Kingdom and the King. She bears two wands. The one in the right turns clockwise and the left turns counterclockwise. The wands represent the forces of involution and evolution which signifies cosmic consciousness or Nirvana. The central fact of this experience is perfect union with the All. They also know that through them the governing and directing power of the universe flows out into manifestation.

Meditation With the World

Picturing yourself as the Tarot card is an immensely powerful meditative technique which can help you get in touch with the consciousness of the path.

- After performing primordial meditation, picture yourself as the androgynous being in the World card.
- You are floating in the sky covered partially in a royal purple scarf that rises above your head and below your feet.
- You have a wand in each hand, going different directions to move energy through the cycles of involution and evolution.

- There is a great green wreath with red ties all around you. You get the sense of a giant ouroboros (the snake eating its own tail).
- You realize that you represent all people of all types.
- You are in complete unity with all aspects of yourself and cosmic consciousness. You are one with nature and the spiritual realms, experiencing complete unity and complete harmony.
- Abide in this state as long as you can.
- When finished, bring yourself back to normal awareness and exit the meditation.

Lilith Consciousness

Lilith's consciousness at this path is your consciousness. If you have embraced her and taken up her transformation you are Lilith embodied. It does not matter what gender identity you see yourself as, you are Lilith's true child and true heir. Her dark light fills you and you are an agent of transformation for yourself and the world.

Lilith Meditation

In the chapter on the Sphere called Crown (*Keter*) we worked with a meditation of unification involving a raven. We will work further with that meditation here on this path.

- Get into a comfortable position.

- Push all thoughts aside and begin to breathe in a regular rhythm.
- Breathe in… and out… in… and out
- As thoughts arise, gently push them aside and refocus on your breathing.
- Picture your heart filled with the dark light of Lilith.
- Envision a sphere of brilliant white light, a diamond-like light that sparkles with rainbow hues, translucent and clear, above your head. Visualize and feel this center of supernal light there, above your head. Awaken this center of divine energy with the intonation of the divine name: *Omoroca* <oh-mo-roc-a>.
- Then envision the light descending through your head down to your throat, forming another sphere of light there, a sphere of translucent lavender light, brightly shining. Awaken this center of divine energy with the intonation of the divine name: Lilith <Lil-ith>.
- Let the light continue its descent down through your body to form another sphere of light in the middle of your torso at your solar plexus, a sphere of translucent golden light that shines brightly like the sun. Awaken this divine center with the intonation of the divine name: Norea <nor-e-a>.
- Envision the light continuing its descent, forming another sphere of translucent violet light at your groin, a vibrant and brightly shining center of divine energy. Awaken this divine center with the intonation of the divine name: Lilit <lil-it>.

- Let the light complete its descent, passing down to your feet and forming a sphere of radiant darkness there, as though a radiant indigo or obsidian black translucent light, all receiving. Awaken this divine center of energy with the intonation of the divine name: Na'amah <nay-ah-ma>
- Having brought Lilith's energy down watch a purple glow fill your entire form.
- Picture your body of dark light floating in the midnight sky. There are stars all around and the moon shines behind you. You can see the earth below you and even though you are high above it, you can see people and animals on the surface with your mind's eye.
- The light of your chest forms into a chalice and turns black. It is a grail containing Lilith's power.
- Picture a black raven flying through the sky. It flies to just above your head and turns to blood red liquid light which pours down through the chakra above your head, through the one at your throat, and then into your heart.
- The black grail fills with the red light and overflows. The red liquid light bubbles up from vast resources and pours down upon the world like a cascade of blood.
- You see the red light cover the earth and spontaneously all beings are filled with Lilith's transformation, becoming their true and authentic selves.
- Abide in this realization as long as you can.

When this is complete return to normal consciousness but bring back the experience of the world's liberation.

References

- Kabbalah and Tarot of the Spirit by Pamela Eakins, Ph.D.
- Qabalah, Qlipoth, and Goetic Magic by Thomas Karlsson
- The Book of Letters by Lawrence Kushner
- Gnosis of the Cosmic Christ by Tau Malachi
- The Essential Kabbalah by Daniel C. Matt
- Wisdom of the Hebrew Aleph*Bet* by Michael L. Munk
- Seventy-Eight Degrees of Wisdom by Rachel Pollack
- Sefer Yetzirah

Made in United States
Troutdale, OR
11/21/2023